Kat Brown is a freelance journalist and commentator whose national work on ADHD, mental health stigma and other social and arts commentary has appeared in the *Telegraph*, *Grazia*, *Woman's Hour* and *The Times*. She is also the author of *No One Talks About This Stuff*, a groundbreaking anthology sharing people's untold experiences of infertility and baby loss.

T0304879

It's Not a Bloody Trend:

Understanding Life as an ADHD Adult

Kat Brown

ROBINSON

ROBINSON

First published in Great Britain in 2024 by Robinson

9 10 8

Copyright © Kat Brown, 2024

The moral right of the author has been asserted.

A CIP catalogue record for this book
is available from the British Library.

ISBN: 978-1-47214-870-4

Typeset in Joanna Nova by SX Composing DTP, Rayleigh, Essex
Printed and bound in Great Britain by Clays Ltd, Elcograf S.p.A.

Papers used by Robinson are from well-managed forests
and other responsible sources.

Robinson
An imprint of
Little, Brown Book Group
Carmelite House
50 Victoria Embankment
London EC4Y 0DZ

An Hachette UK Company
www.hachette.co.uk

www.littlebrown.co.uk

For Ewa S-R, without whom I might never
have known.

And for everyone who first had to self-diagnose to get
a diagnosis. Yes, this is a completely unhinged way of
doing things, but we move!

Contents

Introduction

It's not Father Christmas. It doesn't need you to believe in it to be real.

— ALISON, 51

Author's note

This book is for everyone who is waiting for a diagnosis, as well as for those who are processing the results. A month or so into writing, I got a phone call from the local psychiatric hospital to book me in for an ADHD assessment.

'I'm sorry, there must be a mistake,' I said. 'I was diagnosed in 2020.'

'Oh, how odd,' the disembodied voice at the other end said. 'You're at the top of our list.'

As they talked, I realised that my GP must have left me on the waiting list – a list that, back then, they had told me would take a year, which had still seemed too long to wait. The spiralling wait for an ADHD assessment comes after years of us hiding in plain sight, our GPs and other medical professionals unable to put all the clues together.

I have always tried not to look back. It could be no regrets; it could be not wanting to dwell on the past as I go crashing through it like an elephant in blinkers. In this book, along with the very generous people I have interviewed and the many others who have shared their experiences with me online, I am laying out my own experience quite frankly to show that you are not the only person who has struggled, done stupid things, perhaps succeeded against the odds, and somehow managed to muddle through while knowing that something wasn't quite right. We don't know what we don't know. I have had therapy to process it all before doing this, so, fingers crossed, I can own what I have done rather than melting into shame, but still – this isn't fiction. Be generous to my interviewees, if not to me. Everyone in this book is a real person with worries, hobbies and habits. As you probably have, each has likely boiled a kettle, made dinner in the past twelve hours or stared in a mirror and gone, 'Oh God.'

Trying to find yourself perfectly described here is a wasted task. ADHD is a wondrous constellation that is as specific to the person as their life story, so take what is helpful and sift out what is not. As the recovery saying goes, listen to the similarities and not the differences in the sharing that follows. I wanted to present lived experience alongside interviews with people in the research and clinical fields of ADHD to find answers and explanations and, occasionally, to do a little myth-busting in the space between what the science says about ADHD and what people go through. Sometimes, the science hasn't yet been able to quantify the qualitative data – as regards ADHD and menopause, for example – but focusing on what is proven helps us to live well and combat some of the outrage drivers we see more widely.

'Three's a trend', questions to which the answer is no, and other things I've learned from journalism

When I worked at British *Glamour*, one of my boss's favourite sayings was, 'We're not saving lives here, people,' which continues to be a helpful thing to remember if I'm tying myself in knots about work. I am an arts journalist, copywriter, social media editor, and anything else I can do to pay the bills – I entertain, but I am categorically not saving lives. The boss's other favourite saying, frequently rolled out during pitch meetings, was, 'Three's a trend.' This usually applied to anything on our beats that would be worth turning into a story, and it applies to journalism more broadly, especially online. If an outlet covers a story and it does well – which editors can see because everyone is glued to metrics tools – another will jump on it, then another, until it snowballs, by which point the information and research can start to become a bit sloppy. Things are written up and repeated until they become acknowledged truths, even though that may not be the case.

Where this can become a bit factually spicy is with the 'man bites dog' rule that new journalists are taught about what makes a story newsworthy. A dog biting a man is to be expected and, therefore, not news. A man bites a dog, though – that's a story. It isn't news for a mixed-race woman to experience racism. It becomes news if you can find a source to say that she's lying or – and this is entirely off the top of my head – an ungrateful upstart who has brainwashed a member of the Royal Family. 'Man bites dog' is how we end up with dubious stories, especially in healthcare coverage. It isn't a story to say that millions of people are being misdiagnosed or missed altogether. Where I live in the UK, the National Health Service is under insane levels of pressure; we know this, and nobody likes to suggest that we are not a cutting-edge society. But it is a story if you can find an expert who will say that a condition is being overdiagnosed or overmedicated or that people today are just too pathetic to cope with the vagaries of life. Once you've got that expert, you're free to publish any number of op-eds on the matter, from which you can draw out news stories. Then you'll find more experts wanting their moment in the sun, so you don't need to worry about something as prosaic as an objective truth. Humans adore a big, juicy, gossipy bit of overstatement that feels as though it *should* be true. Of course people are being overdiagnosed! Young people (by which, assume anyone more youthful than the person reading the story, which could be twenty, forty or sixty-five) are too soft for words.

The rise of online news and of people unwilling to pay for its content means that clicks are king. 'A lie gets around the world before the truth has time to get its boots on' – look at Donald Trump. Look at Facebook, Twitter and TikTok. Look at the number of sites erroneously crediting that quote to Winston Churchill.[1] People want to believe what fits with their worldview, often regardless of evidence. Climate change? Those boffins don't know what they're talking about; give me my cheap flights. The same goes for sexual harassment, depression, suicidal thoughts, homophobia, transphobia, sexism, classism and racism. What are they making such a fuss about? We just got on with it in my day.

There are two interesting elements at play here. One is that life is a slog, and people can naturally be quite touchy about the idea of them having had it better or of younger society benefiting from something that they

---

1 In 2021, Dr Oliver Tearle traced the origins of this line to Virgil: 'Rumour, than whom no other evil thing is faster.' The researcher Bonnie Tyler Blake also found that Jonathan Swift punched it up in 1710 as, 'Falsehood flies, and truth comes limping after it.' The *Portland Gazette* followed in 1820: 'Falsehood will fly from Maine to Georgia, while truth is pulling her boots on.' https://interestingliterature.com/2021/06/lie-halfway-round-world-before-truth-boots-on-quote-origin-meaning

did not. Paul Fairie, who researched historical trends in newspaper headlines for his book *The Press Gallery*, has found stories berating everything from workers not wanting to work, children being too soft and men too feminine, to people not being able to take a joke going back every decade to the 1890s. Fairie highlights the public passion for blaming things on new fads, which also ties into that perennial headline staple, 'Questions to which the answer is no', most perfectly exemplified by a headline from 1927: 'Is Jazz Dancing Ruining Legs of American Girls?'

In Western society, we've arguably hamstrung ourselves through our expectations of how a person 'should' be, whether in terms of gender or appearance or how sexuality, identity or disability manifests. Overall, we want the least inconvenience and the maximum productivity for everybody. However, we are in a time of change that is happening incredibly fast. When I was at my thrusting girls' school in the late eighties, we were taught that we could do anything, yet it was barely twenty years since a woman had to be married and have her husband's permission to hold a mortgage. In my lifetime, we have seen abortion made legal in Ireland and rolled back in the US. Future shock, the concept where change happens too quickly for people to catch up, is evident in the clash between progress and fear. Hard-won developments in many social and civil rights areas have led to equality but not enough time for equity to properly bed in. The internet and the twenty-four-hour news cycle have come in in the last thirty years; social media in the last twenty. In barely ten years, we have seen gay marriage in the UK.

Changes to social media have meant equal and constant access to people, news and opinions. As social media and the news cycle shine a light on how little society has progressed in real terms, it becomes preferable to stamp down on someone smaller to make yourself feel significant. Rather than adequately confronting the institutional misogyny that leads to rape, sexual abuse, harassment and the mistreatment of women, gay people and non-white people through every area of society, the focus becomes trans people and 'safe spaces' for women. When every area of society is infiltrated by men abusing their power to abuse people with less power than themselves, how tempting to instead focus on a tiny minority to feel as though you are wresting back some control.

People are also grappling to understand neurological conditions, mental health, physical overlaps, and more. Suppose you have grown up around labels such as awkward, absent-minded, scatter-brained, clumsy, stupid or mental, and have got through life regardless. In that case, you might very well have little time for someone explaining that they are diagnosed with ADHD, autism, EDS or something else. If you don't know someone with that experience, they are 'other' to you already. With social media and online discourse, you are perhaps more likely to dehumanise them because they don't exist in your world. Their reality is not tangible, and so you can assume the worst: that 'they' are just trying to get pills, that 'they' want to decompartmentalise womanhood, that 'they' are just lazy and fat, that 'they' want to take what is yours. Whenever a contrarian voice does come around to a cause, it's usually only because they've found skin in the game, whether themselves or through someone close to them.

The government will pay for injections to prevent obesity because that condition is deemed to reflect poorly on Britain as a country. It's also very visible. This is despite medical professionals and researchers pleading for better access to quality food. In Lambeth, the London constituency where I live, one GP has started to prescribe fruit and vegetables to her patients, which can be collected from various locations in case someone cannot attend the surgery. Rather than prevent, society would instead punish. We hear that the cost-of-living crisis means it's unfair to introduce a tax on ultra-processed and sugary junk food or a watershed on advertising it. There is no talk about subsidies for fruit and vegetables and other healthy nutrition. This focus on visible conditions is again reflected in the growing number of women now being diagnosed with endometriosis, adenomyosis and polycystic ovarian syndrome, all 'invisible' and all of which can affect fertility. A shared symptom is heavy and painful periods, which, for centuries, women have been expected to endure. 'Put up and shut up' is hardly a health catchphrase to be proud of.

When I was at my wits' end trying to conceive, my therapist would help me process pregnancy announcements with the line, 'Good for you, and same for me.' Equality is not a zero-sum game, and neither is equity. Suppose that language is explicitly directed to make someone feel comfortable, or support is given to make their life manageable and bring them up to the base level their neighbour takes for granted. In that case, it doesn't take away from that neighbour. That support generally adds to society in understanding, tolerance and fairness. Removing the stigma around one thing can mean someone feeling comfortable enough to seek help for something else. It doesn't mean more people necessarily claiming that for themselves, but it does mean that people who have suffered for a long time can get the support they need to end their struggle.

Whether in terms of ADHD, depression, autism or trans people, the refrain 'I swear there didn't used to be all this in my day' can be explained by a look at statistics around left-handed people, which is another form of neurodiversity. In 2007, Chris McManus, a professor of psychology at University College London, led a large-scale study of handwriting.[2] He found that the proportion of left-handedness had increased from 3 per cent in the late Victorian era to 11 per cent at the time of the study. McManus said this may be due to a reduced stigma around left-handedness, particularly in attempts to make naturally left-handed children use their right hands. Well into the 1960s, it was widely accepted for children to have their left hands tied behind their backs, and, while now rare, incidences of this are still reported. Historical data on left-handedness are surprisingly rare, to the extent that a museum curator attempting to curate an exhibition on handedness referred to left-handers as being 'a people without a history'.[3]

Perhaps the people we need to convince that ADHD isn't a trend aren't the people out there but 'in here' – even the person writing this book now. Years of feeling defective, less than or a bit 'off' aren't easy to solve, especially when your level of self-trust may not be operating on the level you'd hope for in a mature adult. This is partly why so many people, me included, report feeling deeply anxious ahead of our assessments in case it's found that we don't have it and that we are 'just like this'. ADHD can be, and has been, identified

---

2 McManus, C., & Hartigan, A. (2007), 'Declining left-handedness in Victorian England seen in the films of Mitchell and Kenyon', *Current Biology*, 17 (18)

3 Sadler, N. (1997), 'A sinister way of life: a search for left-handed material culture', in *Experiencing Material Culture in the Western World*, ed. Susan M. Pearce

as many other character traits, best exemplified in the title of Kate Kelly and Peggy Ramundo's 1993 book *You Mean I'm Not Lazy, Stupid or Crazy?!* People with dyslexia were long dismissed as stupid or not trying hard enough. The Deaf community were left behind almost entirely, not least when it was decided to stop using sign language in mainstream schools and force children to lipread. The word 'moron' was invented in the 1900s as one of the classifications for what is now termed intellectual disability. The words formerly used to describe people with Down's syndrome and cerebral palsy are unrepeatable.

We are all adults here. We use our judgement every day. This book reminds us to use that judgement when it comes to ourselves, to question the intention of who is speaking, and not to be swayed by something because it's splashy. To borrow a phrase from the trans community, we have always been here. Mental health or neurodivergent conditions are not new. Being transgender isn't new. Neither is being left-handed, having a learning disability, not having children, being exceptionally short or tall, fat or thin, or having a physical disability. What is relatively new is the understanding of each and the desire to support people with such conditions and attributes in life. Perhaps the difference is feared because it speaks to the deepest concerns of the individual: 'I am the only one who's playing at being a human because everyone else knows what they're doing.' It's easier to squash someone else to make yourself feel more comfortable.

I feel lucky to live in this period of technological development, where I've been able to learn and find other people going through similar experiences. Knowing that things will be leagues better for everybody who comes afterwards has always been a light for me when I'm feeling particularly challenged. That our experiences will help with that is rather lovely to contemplate. Humans are not predictable, but society's response to humans is. You don't know what you don't know. But when you do, it's time to change that narrative and, yes – that trend.

What would you say to someone who didn't 'believe' in ADHD?

PETE, 51: Cool, good luck with that. I'll just be here with a chronic, incurable condition and a solid diagnosis.

ALEX, 40: Just because society hasn't historically recognised or had a name for people who think differently doesn't mean that they haven't always been present. In fact, because of this lack of knowledge, the system has failed so many developing minds by labelling them as disruptive, dreamers or unfocused. It isn't a case of 'lowering the bar to include all people' but changing how we recognise and adapt our judgement of intelligence or societal value in recognition that one system can only ever suit a bell curve of minds.

PHIL, 45: They say people hate change, but really, they just hate adapting to it. It can be hard. Especially for older white males, apparently. It's much easier to dismiss it as 'woke nonsense' and carry on as normal. I don't know why people readily accept that some people's eyes don't work well and need glasses, but find it hard to believe brains work differently. What I do believe is that there is way more neurodiversity in the population than even the scientists realise, and, in time, it'll be a non-thing, like needing to wear spectacles. Visual impairment and treatment in very young children is much better recognised now than it was, and in some cases it can be corrected with very little intervention. Why not ADHD?

NATASZA, 44: Understanding that some people process the world differently is so important. The media has promoted one view of ADHD, which isn't universally true. It's not a deficit of attention but a different way of processing.

ALEX, 43: Someone who resists the idea that ADHD exists has larger issues at hand. It's a shame that they refuse to accept that there are experiences beyond what they personally know. However, others' realities don't cease to exist simply because some people refuse to acknowledge them. Hopefully, they can learn to become more empathetic, even just for their own sake. The world might make a lot more sense to them if they stopped trying to define others without first trying to understand what others are experiencing.

JAMIE, 39: Believe what you want, but don't dismiss someone else's experience. Privilege blinds you to others' suffering.

HELEN, 43: The people who say that are people who don't believe in labels or do the 'Well, we're all a bit like that' stuff: I say that we all go to the toilet, but if we were going to the toilet a hundred times a day then there might be a problem.

SOPHIE, 44: I think anyone who says, 'Isn't everyone a bit like that?' should have the choice between being shot or assessed themselves.

MICHELLE, 41: I'd say to try navigating your way through mental maths in a loud nightclub while making your to-do list without a pen and saying the alphabet backwards while also listening to the same two lines of a song on repeat through one earbud. If your answer is, 'Don't be ridiculous,' I suggest you move on and leave it to the experts. Belief doesn't come into it if scientific evidence corroborates it. I wouldn't wish this on anyone.

HUW, 43: I used to look at the challenges that people with ADHD faced and say, 'That's not ADHD because I have the same challenges all the time, and I'm totally normal.' If you're saying something like that about yourself, maybe there's a reason why you're facing those challenges.

JADE, 34: I can understand why they wouldn't believe in it. So many elements of ADHD contradict one another, so at the surface level, why would you believe in it? It's okay to not believe in something you don't understand as long as you use that as your starting point to actively learn more. I think you would be hard-pressed to find someone who says they don't believe in it after educating themselves on the science rather than deciding based on outdated stereotypes or assumptions about what ADHD is.

ALICE, 40: I don't know that I believe in it either, which sounds bizarre because I'm officially diagnosed with it. I think it's a biological trait that probably was useful in some ways, for women especially, as we were expected to 'gather' while caring for infants. This means ensuring they didn't run off while also looking for berries, listening for tigers, etc. It probably was helpful to us back then, while the kind of hyperfocus that allows some people to stare at spreadsheets for hours might have been detrimental. We've changed the expectation of what our brains should be doing drastically in a very short time, and evolution just hasn't caught up.

FRANCINE, 53: I want people to understand how damaging that attitude can be. I've seen some terrible things happen to people I love who live without support for their ADHD: my daughter had a breakdown, and I see students every day who fail. The stigma against us can destroy lives.

MATTHEW, 10:[4] Do you think that the doctors are lying? Are you one of those weird Joe Rogan supporters?

EMMA, 34: I'd love to show them fly-on-the-wall moments of my life or for them to have a chat with my long-suffering boyfriend!

DEBBY, 35: I'd encourage them to read more about it and approach the subject with compassion. It's difficult to understand something you haven't experienced, but that doesn't mean it isn't real.

ANSHUL, 27: ADHD isn't something you can choose to believe in; it exists. It isn't a negative thing; it just means that our brains work differently, and that's okay. No two people's brains work the same, so ADHD, ASD and other neurodiversities are normal.

---

4 Not an adult with ADHD, but he was very keen to do my online questionnaire and I for one applaud that energy

SARAH, 40: The symptoms and biological pathways are well recognised in science. Almost all conditions are a combination of inherent vulnerabilities and environmental factors. There is little doubt that the rise of smartphones and the disruption of lockdowns have played a major part in the rapid increase in diagnosis over recent years.

CHAPTER ONE
Diagnosis

While idly doomscrolling through Twitter – something I liked to do inbetween breathing and drinking coffee – my brain went ping. An online friend who retweets excellent stuff had shared a thread of adults recently diagnosed with ADHD describing when they first realised they had it.

Being of a generation that loves nothing more than self-knowledge in digestible chunks, I clicked and there it was, that instant recognition. People spoke of suddenly doing badly in work with no explanation as to why, of struggling with fine detail, of no longer being able to 'do the thing', or of talking to friends with ADHD who gave them significant glances or having children or siblings diagnosed and realising the criteria were alarmingly relatable. Others detailed a general sense of fizzing brains, trouble coping, nightmares with money, burnout, extreme fatigue and, above all, a general feeling of spending life trying to navigate an ice rink without skates without letting anyone notice.

I was dimly aware of ADHD and knew it stood for attention deficit hyperactivity disorder. I didn't realise that it had only been named so in the eighties and had been recategorised shortly after, so that rather than focusing on being hyperactive or inattentive, there were now three sub-categories under the ADHD umbrella. Hyperactivity meant symptoms leaned towards problems with impulsivity and hyperactivity; inattentive type (once known as ADD) indicated distractibility and a tendency to daydream; combined type straddled both.

I zoomed through the thread, thinking, 'Yep, yep, OMG yeppp', then read every piece I could find on ADHD, sinking into the harmonious state of concentration that I found so stimulating yet frustratingly difficult to replicate on demand. While I shovelled the contents of Google into my eyes, I learned that ADHD diagnosis in adulthood often follows years of misdiagnosis and treatment for something else entirely. Symptoms would have been present from childhood – it isn't a condition that appears with age like adult acne or the need to go 'Oof' when sitting down. I discovered that many other conditions might come under its overarching umbrella – I had a corresponding list that I'd made shamed trips to my GP to treat over the years, 'yes, it's me – another one' – and that it had a severe impact on a person's ability to focus, to start a task and, confusingly perhaps, to later stop doing said task.

While conversations about ADHD have also been caught up in discussions around ultra-processed food, video games and screens, the earliest descriptions of ADHD in all but name date almost ridiculously far back. The Scottish physician Alexander Crichton documented a condition nicknamed 'the fidgets' by those living with it, which he described in a 1798 textbook and which is a perfect depiction of inattentive-type ADHD:

> In this disease of attention, if it can with propriety be called so, every impression seems to agitate the person, and gives him or her an unnatural degree of mental restlessness. People walking up and down the room, a slight noise in the same, the moving a table, the shutting a door suddenly, a slight excess of heat or of cold, too much light, or too little light, all destroy constant attention in such patients, inasmuch as it is easily excited by every impression.

Until Cambridge researchers discovered Crichton's work, the earliest British descriptions of ADHD-like symptoms were those of Sir George Still, Britain's first professor of paediatric medicine. In a series of lectures to the Royal Society of Physicians in 1902, published later the same year in *The Lancet*, he described the hyperactive variant through studying forty-three children with normal levels of intelligence who experienced problems with sustained attention and self-regulation and were prone to aggression, defiance and excess emotion. Still wrote, 'I would point out that a notable feature in many of these cases of moral defect without general impairment of intellect is a quite abnormal incapacity for sustained attention.' He concluded that 'there is a defect of moral consciousness which cannot be accounted for by any fault of environment'. So much for too many E-numbers or video games, certainly on their own.

I found the modern theories about where ADHD came from fascinating. Some schools of thought had it as a hangover from the hunter-gatherer days when people needed to be ultra-focused on obtaining food. Dr Gabor Maté, who has published several books on ADHD and was himself diagnosed in middle age, is convinced that it is not genetic but rather the result of childhood trauma. ADHD research is moving at such pace that since his book *Scattered Minds* was published in 1999, this theory has been disproven. Research on the overlap in the genes of family members with ADHD has confirmed it as having a heritability aspect of a possible 80 per cent.[5] What is certain is that ADHD is not a mental illness or a question of mental health, as

---

5 Faraone, S. V. & Larsson, H. (2018), 'Genetics of attention deficit hyperactivity disorder', *Molecular Psychiatry*

are depression or anxiety, for example, but a condition and, specifically, a neurodevelopmental disorder, which the International Classification for Diseases defines thus:[6]

> The term applies to a group of disorders of early onset that affect both cognitive and social-communicative development, are multi-factorial in origin, display important sex differences where males are more commonly affected than females, and have a chronic course with impairment generally lasting into adulthood.

That 'chronic' in this context means ongoing is crucial, compared to mood or anxiety disorders, which may be episodic. So, too, is 'impairment'. To diagnose someone with ADHD, their symptoms must be chronic and impair them in multiple areas, such as work, home and social. Let's expand on the video games and Sunny Delight idea of ADHD with this explanation from the UK's official government paper on children with neurodevelopmental disorders:[7]

---

6 Dan J. Stein *et al* (2020), 'Mental, behavioral and neurodevelopmental disorders in the ICD-11: an international perspective on key changes and controversies', *BMC Medicine*

7 Clare Blackburn, Janet Read, Nick Spencer, Annual Report of the Chief Medical Officer 2012, *Our Children Deserve Better: Prevention Pays*; Chapter 9: 'Children with neurodevelopmental disabilities'

Many conditions result from social and genetic factors coming together in complex ways, often across generations. Impairments/conditions resulting from purely genetic or purely social/environmental factors are rare. Common factors include birth weight, age, sex, ethnicity, socio-economic status, parental behaviours, communicable diseases and unintentional injuries.

My mind was truly blown when I started reading about women with ADHD. A 2013 article from the US magazine *The Atlantic* explained how ADHD can present in adult cis women, thanks to the social stereotyping that puts subtle pressure on girls to be polite, quiet and presentable rather than running around causing mayhem. It highlighted how earlier diagnostic criteria were based on investigations with hyperactive white boys. It showed that hyperactivity might manifest in women through racing thoughts or small repetitive movements rather than overt physicality.[8]

My days became soundtracked by podcasts with experts discussing how to work with common ADHD symptoms. I began to sift out the grifters – it is highly unlikely that I want your very expensive course, let alone three adverts for it in one episode – and to have favourite researchers. I adored Dr Ned Hallowell's

8 Yagoda, M (2013), 'ADHD is different for women', *The Atlantic*

strengths-based approach and Dr Russell Barkley's no-nonsense reassurance. Both are American, widely respected, with decades of work in ADHD behind them. The gulf of knowledge between the US and the UK took me back to my pre-internet schooldays when America was the promised land, occasionally throwing us a cultural bone such as *The Simpsons*, Maybelline Great Lash mascara or Oreos, as we otherwise limped through on a six-month delay via Blockbuster rentals and staring at the extortionately priced CD shelves in Woolworth's.

I was sure I had ADHD, but I was worried that my GP might give me the brush-off or think I was trying to get hold of Ritalin to use as a 'smart drug'. At university, I had been prescribed sleeping tablets to treat insomnia, and the doctor only gave me four at a time in case I sold them on – this despite the fact a drug dealer has never approached me in my life, and I would probably approach potential clients nervously going, 'How do you do?' I treated those tablets like jewels and, taking my GP very literally, didn't realise I could ask for the prescription to be repeated, so I never had them again.

Through my twenties and thirties, I'd become used to advocating for myself with medical care. There wasn't enough time for a doctor to put everything together in a ten-minute appointment, and I rarely saw the same person long enough to build a relationship. When I booked an appointment at the surgery to ask to be referred for an assessment, I compiled a file of research on my phone as I have the memory of a goldfish – not early onset Alzheimer's, as I'd been dreading, but – maybe? – undiagnosed ADHD. This GP, one of a floating set who, God knows, had seen enough of me in the years since I moved to their surgery, listened with commendable patience to my TED Talk, then referred me for a telephone consultation with the mental health team, who said I met all the criteria for an assessment, and that they would add me to the waiting list. Success! Briefly. I would have to wait a year.

That seems like nothing at all now, as waiting lists for ADHD assessment for both children and adults are topping four years in the UK. I am a grateful frequent flyer with the NHS, having been on long waiting lists for counselling, binge eating disorder therapy and IVF. But with ADHD, I felt like I had finally cracked what was wrong with me! Getting that rubber stamp that I wasn't a feckless dickhead continually failing at life felt so crucial that I didn't want to wait. I had spent thousands of pounds on exercise, therapy, the 'right' supplements, food and hypnotherapy, which was bloody exhausting. If there was an answer, I wanted to get on with it immediately. This was also highly ADHD.

I returned to my old friend, Google, and typed in 'adult ADHD diagnosis' and was served an ad for a place in London. They had great reviews and, crucially for my mid-pandemic freelancer self with no income beyond the vaccine trial at my local hospital, a Skype appointment was £50 cheaper than in person. I cracked open the pot I set aside for my self-assessment tax payments and transferred several hundred pounds. Since I was diagnosed in 2020, the cost of an online assessment at that clinic has increased by more than three hundred pounds and doubled for in-person.

When my assessment day came, it felt like therapy. I had a ninety-minute consultation with a deeply reassuring psychiatrist, the type of avuncular chap you would be genuinely thrilled to see turn up at your house on your birthday with some balloons and a cake. He took my medical history and listened to the same TED Talk I had given to the GP. Afterwards, he sent me questionnaires for my husband, as someone close to me on a day-to-day basis, and for someone who knew me closely in childhood.

My mum doesn't really believe in mental health, so I sent it to Dad. But he didn't recognise the signs of ADHD in the childhood questionnaire either. A complicating factor was that I was moved up a school year at age seven for being incredibly tall – this is perhaps the most eighties thing ever to have happened – and so any problems were easily explained away as apparent immaturity, and by epilepsy that turned up when I was ten. But also, I was good at school. I performed well, enjoyed extracurricular activities, loved horses, reading and the theatre, and my life was structured through the care and attention of my parents. Other than being comprehensively bullied, my life was pretty sweet.

The next step would usually be for the psychiatrist to go through my school reports as another source of childhood reporting. However, I was thirty-seven, and mine had long been chucked away in the fairly reasonable expectation that I wouldn't need them. I coughed up ninety-nine pounds for a further test called a QB Check. I have stress dreams about exams, but my anxiety about this was off the charts. As with that trip to the GP, so much seemed to ride on it. I was worried about getting it wrong and being sent back to square one without explaining my brain. As much as I didn't want to admit it, my focus on getting a diagnosis was playing into my more damaging habits of throwing money at the problem, not thinking about consequences, and just keeping going, leaning into the gorgeous sensations of chaos, more, now.

The QB Check turned out to be a twenty-minute screen game in which I had to click the mouse when- ever I saw squiggles appear. I was simultaneously worried that I was doing too well and too badly. What if all my years of playing Pokémon meant I was just too good at screen games? Could a person with ADHD be too attentive? Inbetween this fretting, I got bored, then realised that minutes had passed, and I was now wondering if I'd remembered to add chopped tomatoes to the online shopping order.

I handed over another two hundred quid to the clinic for a follow-up appointment to go through the results and held a funeral for my tax account. When my psychiatrist showed me the results, I laughed out loud. The QB Check came back with overwhelming confirmation that I had combined-type ADHD. I felt vindicated, triumphant – normal. I could attack life as everyone else did! The comedian Rachel Bloom, who has since been diagnosed with ADHD herself, describes this feeling perfectly in her song 'A Diagnosis' from *Crazy Ex-Girlfriend* – look it up on YouTube immediately. The rest of my life stretched before me, golden and glorious, and bathed in a glow of understanding.

How did you realise you had ADHD?

CIARA, 29: I've always struggled with executive dysfunction. It's been a vicious cycle of knowing I need to do a thing but sitting around not doing it while being angry at myself for being so 'lazy'. It took a long time for ADHD to occur to me because I didn't have the classic presentation. Although I experienced problems with getting homework and chores done as a kid (and oh boy, did I hyperfocus), I found school easy enough that I was largely able to be successful. It wasn't until university that I started experiencing difficulty staying on top of academics. When I started working from home, there were entire days when I'd sit at my desk and accomplish nothing. I browsed the internet, played with my dog and snacked, but I had nothing to show for my time at the end of the day. This motivated me to pursue a diagnosis earlier this year. I chose to pay for a private assessment because I found the idea of trying to figure out how to navigate all the hoops to get diagnosed through the provincial healthcare system in Canada completely overwhelming. I didn't even know where to start. With the private assessment, all I had to do to set the wheels in motion was to fill out a web form and make a payment. I'm fortunate that the cost wasn't prohibitive for me. I have my diagnosis and report now but haven't accessed medication yet. I have a lot of anxiety about dealing with the medical system, and I have a new GP I've never met. The idea of calling up their office and saying, 'Hey, I've got ADHD! Give me some controlled substances!' is incredibly stressful.

JAMES, 47: I didn't meet my father until I was thirty. We had no contact of any kind. And he said to me once, 'Do you find that when you're doing something, you have to keep stopping and going to do something else? Like, you can't just stick with one task?' It was such an odd thing to say that I brushed it off, but it stuck with me.

Something else got me thinking about ADHD, and I read into it and thought, 'This feels like me.' I remember calling up my dad and saying, 'Do you remember when you asked me this incredibly random question? Did you ask me that because you've got ADHD?' He said yes and that he'd never been diagnosed but always believed that this was something he had. Knowing that it's so hereditary makes a certain amount of sense because that also gelled with me. The more I read up on it, the more I said, 'Oh God, this is absolutely me, all the way through.'

Dad had what a lot of people with ADHD had: he was a bright man with unfulfilled potential. He always felt like he'd hit barriers and could never get past them. He didn't do well at school, couldn't focus, got bad grades, became a truck driver, and was a talented musician and songwriter. He also worked as a croupier at the Playboy Club, but he was a musician for much of his life and then got into sound mixing. He found tasks that suited his brain in that they weren't academic-led but interested him enough to focus on them. Sound engineering worked for him as a music lover because he loved the details. I think he did that thing where rather than 'getting over' or 'learning to overcome' his ADHD, he just found a life that fit in with how his brain was wired.

I've also never been officially diagnosed. I wasn't interested in paying for a diagnosis because I'm not really looking for medication. Talking to my mum is interesting because her dyslexia coloured how she lived her entire life. Only in the last few years have I realised that I've been on a parallel but different track to her, whereby ADHD has been this constant boulder I've been carrying, making everything I do ten times more difficult than it is for a normal person. Without the therapy and the awareness of the diagnosis, you don't have the terminology or the language to express to someone why. My ex-wife thought I was slightly autistic, and before that, she just thought I was fucking rude. It was genuinely amazing she married me. She'd say, 'Why are you so rude to my friends? You're a journalist; you talk to people for a living – what's wrong with you?' I didn't have the words to answer that, but now I have the tools to explain why.

The more you know and the more you're able to understand, the more you're able to explain to other people so that they understand because, without an ADHD brain, nobody has the first clue what it is like to have one. If anyone knew what it was like to live with your brain like this, they would not say [things like 'it's just a trend'] because it's extremely fucking challenging. Explaining it to people on a base level, I just say, 'I'm very easily bored. It's not rudeness. There's nothing I can do about it. Please be more interesting.'

EMILY, 48: I grew up in a really small rural farming community in Canada – like, we got out of school at 2 p.m. so people could go help with the harvest. They didn't know what to do around brain stuff. I remember a guy being diagnosed with dyslexia three months before he graduated from high school. I'm sure it was useful, but he'd struggled so hard by then, so I think school was a little backwards. I had never really heard of ADHD in women, even though I'm very stereotypical. When my daughter was diagnosed, they said it was hereditary, and I was like, 'Shit, I know exactly where she got this from.' It wasn't on anyone's radar, including mine, not even the psychiatrist who eventually diagnosed me. He said that there are so many symptoms that it never crossed his mind until he started reading more about it in his therapeutic practice and that he wouldn't have brought it to me unless I'd brought it to him.

When I read Joanne Steer's *Understanding ADHD in Girls & Women* and got to the bit about what you can expect with undiagnosed ADHD in your late teens and early twenties – the relationships and the risk-taking – it was like a tick box of my life. I got very drunk at twenty, flew to Las Vegas and married someone that I had only been dating for a short time, all of these things that make great stories where everyone's like, 'I can't believe you did that!' and I'm a bit like, 'I can't believe I did that.' But it's exhausting and stressful. My teens through into my early thirties were just chaos: changing jobs constantly, moving all the time, getting bored, changing countries, moving cities, chasing that dopamine. I moved to London because I had a dream that I moved there, so I thought, 'Well, obviously I have to move to London now.' When I think about it logically, there was no job, there was nothing. It was just that I had a dream and decided that was the right thing to do. And yes, it was the best thing, but it's because I made it the best thing, not because it was a really smart thing at twenty-four to go, 'Yeah, let's pack it all in and go to another country!'

CYM, 28: My school report cards always commented on how chatty I was in class. I was voted 'most talkative' in the middle-school yearbook. In high school, I struggled with test taking and classes like foreign languages and history that involved a lot of memorisation – the SAT was a nightmare, and I still have anxiety dreams about it now. I spent almost two years trying to succeed as a chemistry major in college, but I struggled to comprehend and keep up with my classmates. I even pushed myself to attend summer school to avoid falling further behind.

I have been drawn to fast-paced companies where I can juggle several projects simultaneously. I thrive in start-up environments because I am encouraged to help build new processes that allow me to use my strategic thinking and creativity. When I was diagnosed with PMDD (premenstrual dysphoric disorder), ADHD came up a lot. Often, women who have PMDD also have ADHD. I spent several months researching and reading about it before meeting with an ADHD-specialised psychiatrist and being diagnosed. I have felt crazy and lazy so much of my life, but it turns out it was just my brain doing what it knows best. I have been reflecting a lot lately on what this diagnosis means, and I think my biggest takeaway has been that the younger me deserves a huge hug. I think back to all those Spanish and French tests that I had to bring home to get signed because of poor grades, which gave me extreme anxiety; the teachers who pulled me aside and asked if I proofread my papers before turning them in due to the number of careless errors and spelling mistakes, when I knew I had spent hours rereading them; the fear of rejection I had that meant I stayed in unhealthy relationships and friendships for way too long; my difficult relationship with food and how I used it to create dopamine for so much of my life while assuming I just lacked self-control. Present-day me knows so much about myself that I wish the younger me had.

LUDWIG, 29: I really like reading up on things. I've spent hours on Wikipedia, but I never cared for the idea of ADHS[9] because the name is so stupid. I don't have an attention deficit; I just struggle to pay attention to things others want me to pay attention to. I always pay attention to something. I didn't realise what it might be until I was treated for depression, and some of the symptoms got better, but others didn't. It took me six months of self-coaching to accept that I needed professional help, two months to find a doctor who was taking on new patients, and another month waiting for the appointment. From what I heard from other ADHS patients in the waiting room, I was quite lucky: they had driven over an hour to see him.

Going through my childhood and teenage years, it's ridiculous that I wasn't diagnosed earlier. Teachers didn't care that I barely paid attention in class and couldn't keep

---

9 In Germany, ADHD is called ADHS with 'syndrome' replacing 'disorder'

my mouth shut. It had to be my fault that their techniques and strategies failed. I was just an overtaxed child, not understanding how, on the one hand, I was smarter than most other kids, while on the other, I never managed to do any homework and made small, avoidable mistakes. Somehow, I got through, but I'm now in the twentieth semester of a course that's supposed to take ten. My grades are pretty good, and any fellow student will agree that I'm a good chemist and know my subject; I'm just ridiculously bad at setting priorities. Whenever it's time to commit to one thing, I find a new cool topic. This is nothing methylphenidate can fix, but it helps me be more aware of what I plan to do, not forgetting what I'm supposed to work on every time I get distracted. I'm still adjusting the medication, but I already see how much it's helping, and I'm sure that many things would have turned out better for me if I had a prescription earlier.

In my experience, ADHS definitely has upsides, like constantly being interested in new things, noticing things that go unnoticed by others, and randomly hyperfocusing and accomplishing cool things. Having a new hobby every few months is really bad for the budget, though, especially in combination with being impulsive. And randomly hyperfocusing on things is not something you can rely on if you have to pass exams and stick to deadlines. Constantly noticing your surroundings can be tiring. It's not good for mental health to feel guilty for accomplishing less than equally smart people because you have a hard time finishing things up. It's not good for your relationship if you're too tired to do your fair share of chores after a 'normal' working day because life is just ridiculously exhausting if you constantly process everything that's going on around you.

HELEN, 58: Patients really like a doctor with ADHD. Doctors really hate a doctor with ADHD. I was fighting for my sons' diagnoses and treatment before realising I had it myself and being diagnosed at forty-five. I subsequently became a consultant psychiatrist specialising in ADHD, and being able to help so many people has been life-changing. I am so angry at how hard it is for patients to be believed, assessed and treated. Ignore almost everything except fellow ADHDers who get it and what you read in *ADDitude*, and do consider getting a diagnosis because medication and understanding are vital.

ANDY, 52: A friend posted something on Facebook about rejection sensitivity [also called emotional dysregulation]. I read up on it, and thought, 'That sounds very familiar.' It never would have occurred to me in a million years that I had ADHD because I'm a very low-energy dude, and I eventually learned that it is an incredibly bad name for what we have. We don't have a deficit of attention; we pay attention to everything simultaneously, and it's overwhelming; at least, that's how it is with me. When you discover all the checklists, it's like you can see the Matrix. It doesn't mean I can suddenly fix all the problems, but at least I understand them now, which takes a big weight off.

The thing that freaked me out was that there were so many things that all seemed unrelated that turned out to be really common signs of ADHD. I was also stunned by my own ignorance. How can I have lived for half a century without being aware of this? Especially when it's me! With the rejection sensitivity, I do take things too personally. Feeling like I'm disappointing people, not trying hard enough, or people not liking my stuff is just really painful. I don't have a thick skin for that. It's genuinely painful. It's not that I get angry or petty about it; I'm not thin-skinned in that way. I can take a joke; I don't take myself too seriously. I guess it's part of the whole emotional instability. I feel things too strongly, and rejection is part of that.

It's probably one of the reasons why I respond so deeply to stories. People talk about films being emotionally manipulative – that's why I like them. I want my emotions manipulated, and I respond to that, to the point where I could describe a scene and start misting up remembering how it made me feel. It doesn't even need to be particularly emotional. I was trying to describe the plot for The Hunt for Red October to my daughter and started getting all choked up. Like, it's nice, but it's not a tragic romance!

There are so many different overlapping things, even just within ADHD, that the spectrum is three-dimensional. People think it's like IQ that goes from low to high, but it's a constellation, and you can have a bit of this and a bit of the other thing. It's a cloud of possibilities. I wouldn't even know how to categorise the individual expressions of traits, let alone something that encapsulates the whole thing.

A big part of the problem is that they keep changing the criteria, and the tests are all about behaviour. Behaviour is not about what's going on inside your brain; I've spent half a century masking without realising I was doing it because I was pretending to be normal. The questions on the test I took were like, 'Do people often tell you that you do this?' So it's another level removed. And it's like, really? That's the tool you're using to figure out what's going on with this incredibly complex web of neurons in my skull. Like Hannibal Lecter said, 'You think you can dissect me with this blunt little tool?' This is a very, very blunt tool.

HANNAH, 50: Getting diagnosed was a really big step for me. When I came away from it, I remember feeling, 'Oh my God, it's not something wrong with me. There's a reason why I am the way that I am.' As a kid, my parents made me feel as if it was a defect in me whereas, now, I'm able to see myself through the lens of ADHD and have a greater understanding of who I am and why. The psychiatrist who diagnosed me was amazing. He recognised the coping strategies I had put into place, what I had achieved, and who I was, and gave me validation for what I've made of my life considering what I've been through. I felt seen and recognised to have an explanation, to understand myself and also to feel a sense of belonging.

BETHAN, 42: ADHD was something I first thought about in my twenties when I read about it and kept having these light-bulb moments. I spoke to a clinical psychologist friend who said, 'I can't even believe this is a question. How do you not even know by now?' I guess you don't realise your brain is different to everybody else; you think everybody else is running around in the same kind of chaos. I thought, 'All right, that's what I've got.' From a work perspective, I was pretty open about the things I might have challenges with. Still, I didn't realise how detrimental it was to my life until the past few years, and I eventually sought a diagnosis.

The older I got, the harder it was for me to manage my ADHD, which, to be honest, I was not managing in any way before. After hitting burnout three times, I'd worked with a burnout coach in 2021. The first time was really bad. I couldn't open a laptop for six weeks, I spent all my time wandering around parks touching trees, which got me the nickname 'tree pervert' from my boyfriend. I find it so grounding, and I'm always walking around saying, 'That's a good tree.' He finds that hilarious. The second time, I was almost trying to relax into not being burnt out, which is just adding things to your to-do list. The third, I'd taken a month off to rest, recuperate and have a lovely time. I snapped at my boyfriend in the airport, sat on my case and started crying, saying, 'I want to go home.'

This was obviously bigger than work and my over-working to compensate for the constant people-pleasing. I knew there was something beyond that here, and it was time to get a grip on it. I was always such a twat to myself. A lot of the time, I was a shitter boss to myself than anyone else because I was trying to prove something or working on things that I wasn't good at when somebody else could be. Compared to now, post-diagnosis, I would say horrible, unkind things to myself. I still catch myself now and again, but the diagnosis has completely changed my life and how I speak to myself and about myself to others. I feel more relaxed just having had it. Before, I was living in high stress. I still get like that, but far less often. I'm kinder to myself than I ever have been, and it comes across in who I am to other people. I'm more content so I'm not as much of a knob.

THE PROFESSIONAL VIEW

DR SHYAMAL MASHRU is a consultant psychiatrist in an ADHD service in the NHS and private practice. He also works with patients who suffer from general psychiatric conditions including depression, anxiety, OCD, PTSD, psychosis and personality disorder.

For diagnostic classification purposes, the hallmarks of ADHD are two categories of symptoms: **inattentive** and **hyperactive/impulsive**. Some people present with both, and some present primarily with one.

The **combined subtype** applies to about 85 per cent of adults with ADHD, with inattentive, hyperactive and impulsive symptoms. Then there is **predominantly inattentive subtype**, which used to be called ADD (attention deficit disorder). That term was purposely changed because people with that subtype will quite commonly have certain features of hyperactivity and impulsivity. In adults, excessive energy goes inwards and becomes mental energy that causes overthinking and excessive mind wandering, leading to high anxiety rates. People start to ruminate; they have different thoughts rushing in and out all the time, and while they can get hyperfocused on tasks, at other points, they're just thinking of twenty different things that need to be done. Then, they get almost paralysed, leading to procrastination and anxiety.

The rarest in adults is **predominantly hyperactive subtype**. The main clinical presentation is physical fidgetiness, restlessness, being very loud, exuberant and extremely talkative, and impulsivity symptoms like impatience and struggling to wait that can happen in physical settings like a queue or by jumping into conversations or blurting out answers before questions are complete. One explanation could be trying to get their point across quickly, but from speaking to patients – and I've seen four thousand now, at least – it's often because they're worried they'll forget what they're going to say. With excessive mind wandering in conversations, someone may have thought of something that was said a few minutes ago, so when they come out with things, it's not always following the narrative, and the other person feels confused.

We also see a gender difference. While most adults – men and women – are diagnosed with combined type, we tend to see more women within the percentage of the inattentive type. This is a lot of the people that we're seeing in both private practice and the NHS, the people that were missed because many had social anxiety and didn't present as disruptive. They were the ones sitting in the back of their classroom doodling, looking out of a window, lost in their thoughts.

Clinicians are realising it's not an attention deficit but more of an attention dysregulation. Attention deficit suggests that you can't concentrate, but it's more that you can't appropriately hone your attention, so it's like the radio signal's tuning into everything. With certain things you are interested in, you can go into extreme concentration to the point where some people forget to eat, drink or even go to the toilet. Some people have then used that to their advantage to become very successful.

Because the emotional element of ADHD is not currently part of the diagnostic classification, there's a risk that a proportion of people are being prescribed incorrect medications. Suppose you don't know that 70 to 80 per cent of people with ADHD have anxiety and depression because of it, potentially because of low dopamine, low noradrenaline and other lifestyle stuff. In that case, you're potentially putting them on an antidepressant to increase their serotonin levels, which will have some emotional numbing effect, if anything. It's like putting a plaster on, but the bleed is internal. You're still bleeding away in there, but it doesn't look like you're bleeding out. It hasn't got to the root of the problem.

PROFESSOR PHILIP ASHERSON has been a senior member of the UK National Adult ADHD Clinic at the Maudsley Hospital in south London since 1998 and co-authored the 2008 NICE guidelines on ADHD with Professor Susan Young. He co-founded the UK Adult ADHD Network for professionals. His work at King's College London includes clinical, quantitative genetic and molecular genetic studies of ADHD in adults and children and clinical assessment and treatment of adult ADHD.

The key question everyone should ask is: do I have a core problem with my attention? They may also have the core problem of being too restless and a bit impulsive; they may not. It's good for people to know that some have that more than others, and some don't. However, almost everyone with ADHD has this core attention problem – do they feel that that's underpinning any other issues that they experience? Another question to ask: am I somebody who really feels I need help? Because part of the diagnosis is that you're impaired. One way to define that might be as something that's impacting me in a way that I'm finding difficult or distressing, or something I can't cope with and need help for. You're impaired if you think you're impaired. If you're very high-functioning, other people might look at you and say you're not impaired, but that can often be because they're not seeing the more hidden aspects of ADHD. One common perspective is to ask how someone can have ADHD if they don't look restless, aren't talking too much, and appear to be able to focus on some things. This ignores the huge efforts people have to make in their daily lives to keep on top of things and to focus. The impact on them might include feeling stressed or fatigued and not sleeping, not being able to rest properly, which they may well be able to mask in common with many other problems.

The impact that ADHD has on individual people can vary, and that is partly the severity. You're much more likely to think of it as a disorder if it is very severe. But also, some people are more skilled at adapting or have a more positive outlook. Perhaps they had more support growing up, whereas others have had more negative experiences. There may be all sorts of factors that explain why some people manage life with ADHD better than others. However, just because some people manage it really well, you can't then say that everyone can. That wouldn't be fair, and some people really don't. The first step with exploring all this as an adult is to see what's out there and whether it makes sense to you – and this also applies to people who aren't sure, either about themselves or about someone else. If you have a relative being treated for ADHD, they might allow you to go and see their doctor with them, who could then help explain it further. People often bring their partners, or even their parents, into our service, and having those conversations with everybody can be helpful. Ultimately, if people respond to the treatments they're being offered, it can become more evident to others that something is changing.

DR TONY LLOYD is the CEO of the ADHD Foundation, Britain's leading charity for ADHD research, awareness and support. He is a psychotherapist and coach and has co-authored national reports on ADHD and neurodiversity.

I was twenty-nine when I looked up ADHD on the NHS website and thought, 'That's not me.' You see that people with ADHD are more likely to abuse drugs, be alcoholics and engage in criminality and think, 'Oh, my God, this is horrific.' Yet there's the other side of ADHD: look at all the research from Stanford about university graduates with ADHD being twice as likely to start their own business and that over 30 per cent of entrepreneurs have either ADHD or dyslexia, or both. These were the people we used to call workaholics. We never said they had ADHD because 'successful people' don't have ADHD, dyslexia or autism. I'm not being funny but look at politics. Reframing the thinking is key. We do a lot of work in business talking to boards and senior leadership, and there's this *Spartacus* moment where they all start raising their hands: 'I'm dyslexic,' 'I've got ADHD,' or 'My kids have it.' A faculty chair will say, 'I can't possibly have special educational needs; I've got three PhDs!' I'd say, 'Well, what do you think a special educational need is?' At some point in our lives, we all have one because life events, trauma and loss impair our cognitive functioning.

We've now got this tide of adults realising. Look at Stephen Fry; he was initially diagnosed with bipolar but now has a diagnosis of ADHD. We've got to destigmatise it because ADHD is not the naughty, fidgety boy who will end up in jail – even though quite a few of them do. I'm not anti the medical model at all – I use meds – but as soon as children reach the age of reason, we're telling them they are not able and are different when everybody in school has to be the same. The contrasting irony is that the diversity of human neurocognitive capabilities is the universal design. Nobody on this planet looks the same, sounds the same and has the same brain, yet we have this arbitrary thought of a majority, and anybody who's not a majority is abnormal or doesn't belong. It's permeated our culture regarding how we've thought of people of colour and LGBTQ. Until the late fifties, if you were a mixed-race child in this country, you were still classed as educationally subnormal. If that isn't eugenicist in undertone, I don't know what is. What we have going on now is an evolutionary awareness. For all social media's problems, it's been very democratising.

INDER, 59: The diagnosis journey has been pretty poor so I've done a lot of self-help and self-learning. About nine years ago, I went to see my GP and said, 'Look, there's something wrong with me. I've never been able to concentrate. I've never been a good learner. I'm not a good listener. That's hampered me all the way through.' The GP, a friend, said, 'Don't be silly, pull yourself together. Don't come to me with excuses; you're supposed to be a man. Just take it. You haven't got ADHD.' I left it at that.

I came to the UK from India when I was four. I had to pick up English, which I did piecemeal as I've never been able to learn or concentrate. My parents didn't give a toss about my education or learning English, yet they'd say, 'This bloke's a doctor, and we want you to be one, too.' How will I be a doctor if I can't read and write properly? They wanted the old Indian mentality: we're staying at home, you're staying in the family, and you've got to pay into the pot, so I never had any money to spend. My dad was against rugby because I had to pay match fees, even though I was earning. It was a horrible childhood. My parents both worked, so I took my younger brothers to nursery, picked them up after school and cooked their food because my dad worked the night shift and didn't wake up until five or six o'clock. That's bloody tough for a nine-year-old. I've never had any breakfast in my life. That's why I don't eat breakfast now.

When I started secondary school, they branded me a complete thicko and put me in the bottom set. The thing that stood out was that I was quite exceptional at history. I came in second in the year, but I couldn't take my qualifications because I was in the bottom set. I left school at sixteen and became a welder, which I absolutely hated. I was still playing rugby, and a guy from the club came back from his PhD at Cambridge and invited me to join a class he was teaching so I could do my O and A levels. I could speak proper English but couldn't read or write it, so I went off and learned that it was 'the cat sat on the mat', not 'cat sat mat'. I did my exams, and he wrote me my university reference. To this day, I don't know what's a noun, an adverb or an adjective, but I'm a lawyer, and I write perfect English. I have to, or I'd get sacked.

After taking voluntary redundancy in 2008, I became depressed. The rugby club chairman visited and asked me to do some work for him. Then he got me more work and said I had to become chairman of the youth section in return. It kept me sane, really. I was also coaching because my son was a player, and I saw some hyper children. I spoke to their parents, who told me they suspected they had ADHD. When I saw these kids, I remembered how I was. I did some research and started putting it together.

I look back at it all and think, 'How the hell have I managed?' My wife says it's tenacity, getting up again after so many falls, but I got tired of that eventually. I didn't care if I lived or died. I'd made a lot of money, so I paid off the mortgages and everything so my family wouldn't have any worries financially. And then I thought, 'That's it, I've done my part. If I'm still around, fair enough; if I'm not, who gives a fuck?' That's what got me looking into ADHD again because I realised there must be something going on. ADHD wasn't covered by my work's private healthcare so I went back to the GP because I couldn't cope. Three of my friends had committed suicide. One was a very successful person with three kids. I thought there must be a reason why they did that, but people were calling them selfish, and I had that mindset. I said I'd never do that while my kids are young. That's one of the reasons I put all the money away. I did everything just to get it all ready. I didn't do it because I'm too strong, but even sometimes, my patience wears. When I went to the doctor's office, I said, 'Look, I'm having suicidal thoughts.' He asked what I wanted him to do, and I asked him to refer me for an ADHD assessment, which he did. Then things changed with my work healthcare, so I got a faster appointment.

[Inder was diagnosed with ADHD through his work's health insurance a week after our first conversation.] After the initial shock things have definitely improved. Now I know why I do things and why I am a bit 'that way'. I have also created a mental 'pause button' that really helps. With the diagnosis, I have begun to cope.

Cheatsheet: A Brief Summary of ADHD

Types of ADHD and typical symptoms

Hyperactive-impulsive: The 'classic' idea of ADHD and the least common in adults: impulsive behaviour, risk-taking, chronic impatience, restlessness and interrupting.

Inattentive: Formerly known as ADD until researchers found that hyperactivity manifests internally. Easily distracted, has difficulty following instructions and completing tasks, has racing thoughts and rumination, and often mislays things.

Combined: A delightful cocktail of the two; 85 per cent of adults with ADHD are diagnosed with combined type.

Treatment recommendations

A three-pronged approach of medication, general therapy and behavioural therapy (ADHD coaching), with support from lifestyle factors: regular exercise, nutritious meals, good sleep hygiene, time spent in nature, limiting alcohol, nicotine and caffeine, healthy work and relationships.

Types of medications

Stimulants (methylphenidate and amphetamine): These stimulate the amount of dopamine and nor-epinephrine to increase focus and working memory and manage impulse control. (Unmedicated people with ADHD may also find that 'uppers' such as caffeine or speed have little to no effect on their brain.) Stimulant medication comes in instant-release and extended-release variants and effectiveness is noted immediately. Medication passes through the system quickly leaving no residue. 'Ritalin' is a familiar brand name, but medication is often packaged using the chemical name.

Non-stimulants (atomoxetine): Results may take several weeks to become evident, but this can be a stable way of achieving long-lasting effects, especially in patients with pre-existing addiction issues, or who experience significant side effects with stimulants.

Key terms

Comorbidity: Two or more conditions occurring at the same time.

Differential diagnosis: Where there is more than one possibility for your condition and your doctor must differentiate between them to establish which is correct.

Emotional regulation: The ability to manage feelings appropriately, sometimes known as rejection sensitivity or rejection sensitivity dysphoria, although these terms are not medically recognised.

Executive function: The mental skills that help you get things done, or 'adulting'.

Hyperfocus: An intense concentration locked on to a particular activity, event or research topic.

Pre-Payment Certificate: This NHS godsend costs just over £100 for the year – compare that to just under a tenner a month for a single medication, let alone multiple – and you can pay by monthly direct debit. Order it online to cover your NHS and shared-care prescriptions.

Stimming: A term borrowed from the autistic community, this constant movement is a way that hyperactivity can manifest through fidget toys, chewing gum or repeated body movements, including self-harm.

Working memory: The brain system that temporarily stores and processes information for more complex tasks.

Diagnosis pathways

HEALTH SERVICE

- Your first step is to see your GP or primary care physician. You don't need to have a file of evidence, but given the short time you have in an appointment, it would be useful to give them a clear idea of why you want to be put forward for an ADHD assessment.

- Your GP may immediately put you on the waiting list for assessment, or you may have a follow-up phone call with a mental health team to discuss this in a longer conversation.

PRIVATE

- A word-of-mouth recommendation from someone you trust is helpful. Your assessing consultant should also work in the NHS. The assessment appointment should be at least ninety minutes, not counting pre- and post-assessment questionnaires, to give your consultant time to properly take your history.

- Factor in post-assessment costs like regular consultation charges and medication.

- It is much – much – cheaper to get a private prescription fulfilled at your local pharmacy than through a snazzy same-day delivery service.

RIGHT TO CHOOSE

- Since 2018, patients in England can use **Right to Choose** to be assessed online, without payment, through any NHS-approved organisation. However, apply the same criteria as you would to a private firm, and your GP must refer you.

CHAPTER TWO

Acceptance

Self-acceptance has been arguably my most challenging element of ADHD diagnosis and is an ongoing process. I wish I could give you my hard and fast tips for accepting yourself, in an afternoon, five easy stages, ten foods you must eat for self-acceptance; but to be completely upfront, it's a shit show. I realised I was confusing it with self-care, as though I could bathe myself into a state of equanimity if I only threw enough Olverum into the tub with the Epsom salts. My diaries from the last ten years are filled with references to accepting myself, mainly in terms of it being something I have to learn or master — and by diaries, I mean the Notes app on my phone, the only thing I am guaranteed to have on me.

Whenever something significant and positive has changed for me, it's usually felt like something I've had no control over. When I started running, and then long-distance running, it felt like the right moment because it didn't feel like I was doing it; it had become something I did. I would know the right moment had come because I'd be overcome by the joy of being possessed by a mission. When I got my diagnosis, I felt joy at having an explanation, but nothing changed. I was still me, but now I was infinitely more aware of my habits and traits in a way that overpowered me. I was four months into therapy, specifically around ADHD, when I had my left hip replaced. The operation went well, but the wound became infected. After a second, less pleasant, operation to clean it out, I was on antibiotics for three months, which meant I could barely work and, as I am self-employed, my husband shouldered the brunt of the finances and housework. I could have made peace with this more quickly had I developed self-acceptance. However, I was still wildly raw about the ADHD, about not being able to work, and about my husband having to support us both during the pandemic and when infertility sent me into mad chaos. I had spent years believing that I couldn't ask anyone for help or I would inconvenience them, and now I was four years into my husband having to take 'in sickness and in health, for richer or poorer' pretty bloody literally. Incidentally, his was a textbook example of how not to make your flailing partner feel bad – all the bad feelings were my guilt and shame. If I were better or different, this would not be happening. I would be pulling my weight. I would not have a brain made entirely of golden retrievers and candyfloss. Rebuilding my strength and picking up more work has helped me reach a state of mind where I can contemplate self-acceptance. Practically, reading and listening both to experts in the field and to people with ADHD helps more than I can say. I just am. You just are. We just are. It's ADHD, for good and for ill, and we can reclaim dignity in that by actively learning how best to live with it.

PROFESSIONAL VIEW

PROFESSOR SUSAN YOUNG is a clinical and forensic psychologist. In 1994, she and Dr Brian Toone co-founded the UK's first adult ADHD clinic at the Maudsley Hospital. She has delivered clinical treatment programmes for children, adolescents and adults, now provided globally, and has published over 150 papers on ADHD and neuro-diversity. In 2008, Professor Young co-authored NICE Guidelines on ADHD, laying out adult ADHD in Britain.

When people get a diagnosis, they go through a process almost like a bereavement. They look back and get angry because it's been missed, and they have spent all their lives feeling misunderstood. By the time they're an adult, they've often told their story to many people, and everyone's missed it. There have been opportunities. It's not like it's the first time they've pitched up and said, 'Hey, you know, something's not right.' I picked this up because I've worked in the world of

ADHD for many, many years, and I've worked so psychotherapeutically with people. People were being referred for psychological interventions for strategies to help them organise and manage their time, to help them plan and motivate themselves, and to help them in their work. I'd written the book on it, so they'd come to me, and I discovered that I couldn't help them with the strategies and planning until they'd gone through the bereavement stage. I had almost to put everything down, sit back, and say, 'Let's talk about the past.'

Until you've helped them to get through these stages of acceptance, you can't do the standard CBT to help with strategies, any of that. It's an emotional process. First of all, it's relief, then it's anxiety about the future, and then it's anger about the past. Then there's hope that things will change, and we usually go on to medication. For many people, that changes everything, but for a sizeable proportion, it doesn't. But I think there's a disappointment for all of them because pills don't build skills. You can think medication is a panacea that will change your life. It doesn't change the loss of achievement or opportunities until you help someone work through those stages and get to a state of accommodation where they accept themselves as an ADHD person and accept what's happened; then they can move on. That's a critical process that they need to be helped through. It's absolutely no good trying to give people strategies for time management and social skills at that stage because they're revisiting the past and reframing who they are. People do need to heal. When you get a diagnosis for the first time in adulthood, that's where the journey starts.

One of the key tools in this is psychological treatment, but as it's difficult to access on the NHS, it's unavailable to most people. Those who can afford it may go privately, but most people don't; they're in turmoil at that stage. Everyone will heal over time from some difficulty in life. You could take clinical depression: even without treatment, people will heal from that eventually. It's not something that, once you have it, you have it for life. People will heal. It just takes such a long time. It's like taking something down off the shelf. If you take it down and look at it, turn it around and polish it a bit, you can get the feel of it. You get to understand it. It becomes more familiar. Then you can start to accommodate and accept it.

You start asking a billion and one questions in your head that no one else asks because it doesn't occur to them.

– MICHELLE, 41

How did you feel about realising you had ADHD?

CLARE, 61: I learned about ADHD through my niece's diagnosis and realising it explained me almost completely. I recognised my dad was a classic case. Our family refers to time versus 'Dad-time', and my mother always said he didn't have a memory but a forgettery. It's helped me forgive him for so many things I now realise he couldn't help. I don't hate or beat myself up as much and try to find ways to engage my brain even if it's only at a basic maintenance level while I'm waiting for its engine to turn over.

EVELINE, 31: I've had a late diagnosis – last autumn here in Beirut and January in my home country, the Netherlands. Doing an assessment and starting therapy in two countries and cultures has been fascinating. Getting to the point of diagnosis has been hard and took a long time. I am still coming to terms with the impact of it on my life (and what a difference earlier knowledge on this could have made) and am now navigating starting medication, having therapy and how to deal with this in the rest of my life. For now, I realise the sheer necessity of self-acceptance in a world that often won't accept me for who I am and how I function. It is not easy, but life gets much more bearable if you are at least not judging yourself for something that is part of who you are. The first step is to be nice to yourself.

JEN, 41: It's a very difficult one to get your head around. I keep thinking maybe I don't even have it, maybe I'm just a nightmare. The symptoms can be explained as character flaws, and there's no 'test' or scan that can give you certainty, so it's a huge mind-bender. I have to keep reminding myself, 'Jen, your daughter has Tourette's, ADHD and dyslexia; your dad is severely dyslexic; your brother once lost twenty-three iPhones in one year, and your mum cannot close a cupboard door. Allow yourself the luxury of brain science!'

ANDY, 52: Jessica McCabe interviewed someone about late-life diagnosis on her YouTube channel, and he described it as almost like going through a period of grief. You look back and think, 'If only I'd known all this about myself when I was ten, how different my life could have been, how much happier I could have been, or more productive'. You would have made different choices. And it's true; it felt a lot like grief, but that didn't last because the past is the past. I've got the rest of my life, so I can make better choices moving forward.

It would be easy to fall into that hole of, 'Oh my God, I've wasted my life', kind of thing. The fact is things are good. I have a good life. Good job. I've got a great family. Forgiving yourself is a part of that. I always beat myself up because I thought everybody was right when they told me I wasn't trying hard enough or was stupid or lazy, because it takes a toll. It was more like realising that I had nothing to forgive myself for. I'd spent my whole life being told I was failing, and actually, I literally have a neurological disorder. Considering I've been carrying that for half a century, I think I'm doing pretty well!

MICHELLE, 41: I get emotional when talking about this. The relief knowing that there was a reason for the degrees I didn't finish, that I get bored easily and I find it hard to clean my house at certain times of the month. I felt like a failure as a human being or an adult woman. The grief comes when I think of all the things that have happened to me, that I've done, the relationships I've lost, and the chances I have not taken. That person twenty years ago, had she known this was a thing, maybe she would have done something different. I love my job, but I did so many things I didn't enjoy. I put up with people demeaning me or feeling like I wasn't good enough.

Looking back at my education and my hobbies, you start to wonder, 'What's my personality? What's the ADHD? And autism?' Which part caused this? Is it me, or is it not me? And then you start to question your identity. Were you always supposed to be like this? What if you weren't like this? How do other people do stuff? You start asking a billion and one questions that no one else does because it doesn't occur to them. 'Relieved and aggrieved' is the mantra I have right now because I'm going to keep on through that cycle until one day, hopefully, I'll think, 'All right, I can do this now. Let's go do life'.

OCTAVIA, 50: I was insulted when a peer at psychotherapy college first suggested ADHD, but I would never have finished my course without the diagnosis and understanding why I struggled when others didn't. I have a deeper understanding of myself now and grieve that I never knew when my mum was alive, as it caused friction in our relationship. She probably had ADHD, too. I'm now working with clients at various stages of diagnosis and am also seven years sober. Addiction and eating disorders are part of my history. Everything makes sense now.

ANNABELLE, 51: A lot of people told me about the grieving process when you get diagnosed, and I'd say, 'I'll be fine. I've been through worse!' but it *was* really hard. There were so many what-ifs. I felt so lonely. I'd felt that everybody in the rooms[10] was getting on with their sober life, but something inside me still wasn't right. I stopped talking to people I loved because I didn't know how to explain what was happening. How do you explain what ADHD is when you don't know what you've got? I became more and more isolated until I got the diagnosis.

EMILY, 48: If I let it, there is an immense sadness when looking at my life. How much more security could I have had? How much more self-love could there have been? How many more jobs could I have found more rewarding? I look at my daughter and think, 'You're going to get to enjoy those things in a more stable way than I did.' That, combined with therapy and a better understanding of who I am, means I don't need to keep beating myself up, and if I'm

---

10 Slang term for being active in a recovery programme

the happiest seventy-two-year-old woman in the world, I'll be the happiest seventy-two-year-old woman in the world.

SEAN, 38: I have trouble referring to it as a disability because I don't feel it's legitimate enough, which is probably really stupid. There are many times when I'm like, 'Oh, I'm able to do this because of my ADHD; this is why I'm good at doing ten different things.' It's not the same as not being able to walk. You shouldn't compare yourself, but there's definitely that feeling that sometimes it's a good thing, so I feel weird calling it a disability, and then that leads to not looking for the help I probably should be getting because of all the things I am struggling with.

SARAH, 31: I was always good academically, and I've always been able to think logically. Subjects which let me learn rules as shortcuts to answers, like maths, chemistry, biology or computing, were easy, but anything which required less defined rules, or memorisation, such as languages or history, was harder. I've always struggled with memory and habits. While I didn't match the popular view of ADHD as I did well in exams and was quiet in class, traits such as forgetting books (so keeping them all in a very heavy bag), daydreaming and being untidy were explained as being disorganised, quiet or lazy. I've always felt like my brain worked a bit differently. Things didn't work the way I wanted them to. I would try resolutions and new ways of organising myself, tell myself I'd really try this time, and then it would gradually crumble. I learned that, because I didn't seem to care enough to maintain these things, I must be happy with not doing them. I didn't realise until hearing about ADHD in women on a podcast that maybe things weren't okay that way, and I should ask for help. While realising through diagnosis and support that these things are due to my brain and cannot be changed but can be worked with, I've let go of some of the guilt and shame I've kept over the years. Two things have helped. First, medication has been life-changing. I still forget to take it, and my wife notices more than me if I have forgotten. Still, it's allowed me to be so much more present in my daily life. Second, my wife's support underpinned by an incredibly supportive and open community. I've understood myself more when learning about how my brain works and communicating it better. They've given me the words, and my wife has sought to understand these words.

CLARE, 42: You sometimes want people to know – even people from the past that you don't speak to or care about any more – that all that time you gave me grief for this, that and the other, it wasn't my fault. So you know, up yours! It's that whole thing of not all disabilities being visible. One of my friends said, 'Do you get a blue badge now?' Sadly not! I thought that'd be nice because I can't park for toffee, but why should you struggle in situations where you're entitled not to struggle? We're going to Disney in

August, and my son and I are entitled to the Disability
Access Pass because of our ADHD. You can book two rides
in advance where you don't need to queue. I *can* queue. I've
queued before, but ADHD is covered for a reason, so I will
use it, and if that's a bit of a gain for the things that have
been hard over the years, then we'll take it. Same with
Access to Work.[11] 'Oh, you're getting all these things.' I've
paid my taxes for it over the years and all the interest to
my banks and credit cards, so I will take it.

NATALIE, 33: Since the diagnosis, I've been on and off
medication and have regular sessions with an ADHD coach
via Access to Work. I speak with my coach every couple of
weeks, and just having a kind, well-informed professional
listen to my challenges and provide some coping strategies
has been so beneficial. I'm reading ADHD: An A–Z by
Leanne Maskell, which is great. I was diagnosed less than
two years ago, so it's all still a bit raw – I also spent a lot of
last year feeling extremely angry, frustrated and, honestly,
just deeply sad about the fact I'd been undiagnosed all
these years. I couldn't help but go through all the traumatic
events in my head and question whether they would have
happened had I been diagnosed sooner. I'm sure this is
very common. I think I was grieving a lot last year, but
this year, my focus is on being kinder to myself, arming

---

11 Access to Work is a government scheme in the UK offering grants to people with
physical or mental health conditions to help them stay in work. The grants are
available to employed and self-employed people

myself with more knowledge and trying to put some of these strategies in place to make my life easier.

DR TONY LLOYD: I say I'm neurodiverse and have ADHD. I'm not 'ADHDic', as you might be dyslexic, and many people with autism will say, 'I don't have autism, I'm autistic.' It doesn't define my identity. It is a part of who I am, but my personality, my values, my ethics, my life experiences, the love, the support, the kindness that I've had from people, particularly at some very crucial stages in my life, have all played a very significant part in my becoming who I am and therefore who I am is Tony. I don't introduce myself by saying, 'Hi, I'm Tony, I've got ADHD,' or, 'I am ADHDic,' but it's generational, like how we say LGBTQ. I've lost track of all the acronyms; I just think, 'Great, good for you.' We don't all fit into one box, and don't be afraid to disappoint people if you don't fit into their boxes. People challenge me about not identifying as 'neurodiverse', but the dictionary definition is that you're either 'neurodivergent' or 'neurotypical', which creates dichotomies where we're othering people. Why do I have to identify with a word where the aetiology is 'deviant, deviating from the norm'? I don't refer to my friends of colour as 'racially divergent'. I don't identify as 'sexually divergent' because I'm married to a man. It's an evolving language and an evolving conversation. Look at the words we used to use for people with disabilities (which is another word I don't like). We used to call them invalids. Invalid.

An invalid human being. I've been called ableist because I don't consider myself disabled. I was disabled, but I was disabled by school and by a medical model that views any human being who has any struggle or impairment purely through the lens of pathology and deficit rather than recognising that, while ADHD undoubtedly comes with some challenges, it's also inevitably part of where I've been very successful. But then, define success because for me, and forgive me if it sounds trite, the only thing people ever remember you for is whether you were a kind person, not how many letters you had after your name, what your job title was or how wealthy you were.

CHAPTER THREE

Comorbidities

Realising you have ADHD feels like the end of a crime show where the detective comes out and says, 'Just one more thing . . .' It's incredible how the threads come together. I wondered how it could be so badly missed, especially given my reasonably frequent contact with doctors, but if you don't know that there is a bigger picture you could be looking for, then I suppose it's just bad luck. I felt greedy, potentially a hypochondriac, for having so many conditions. I'd sing them to the tune of the 'Fast Food Song': 'ADHD and BED, insomnia, depression and anxiety.' It's only when you list them out loud that it hits you that you are dealing with a lot. Until then, it's just you, drifting along in your head, feeling terrible and thinking this is entirely normal.

Given that I went to school in Britain in the eighties and nineties, it's unlikely I would have been diagnosed with ADHD, but the circumstances that ran alongside my schooling meant that the chances became even slimmer. When I was six and cheerfully towering over my classmates by at least a head, my height was unusual enough for my parents to consult doctors who recommended that I either be given hormones to stunt my growth or moved up a year at school – there was no option three. It's completely mad, but it was the eighties. Maybe they were all on cocaine, although I'm not sure whether cocaine made it out as far as New Malden. In any case, I was moved to a new school at seven. I don't know what difference they thought this would make. Nobody caught up to me height-wise for years, and it just meant I missed a year of socialisation and learning the codes that schoolchildren use instead of plain speaking. I just floated along without any of that classroom etiquette until I hit the abrupt boundaries of senior school.

At ten, I was extremely tall, had red hair – considered a crime in the nineties – and loved showing off. I was indoctrinated by Enid Blyton and pony books, so my moral compass was that of a middle-aged woman in the 1960s rather than set to deal with a contemporary school. I also developed petit mal epilepsy, which caused absence seizures where you blank out mid-conversation, and the meds seemed to turn my hair from reasonably straight to unmanageably frizzy. Children can smell difference like a shark smells blood, and certain types will circle accordingly. All these factors came together in a storm of bullying. Any chance of an ugly duckling to swan evolution ended when I fell off my bike and landed on my face, my broken teeth jammed back in and held together with NHS ingenuity and a paperclip. I got a card in the post from my class, with the cartoon bear that dominated so much nineties stationery standing by a little garden gate and waving under a printed 'We miss you' message. Someone had done a little graffiti scribble on the gate, an added flourish I appreciated until I peered closer and saw the word 'not' still faintly visible under layers of biro. When I returned to school, I was christened 'RoboGob', a peerless nickname given the circumstances: 10/10, no notes. Being bullied was almost easier when it was stereotypical – girls from the year above throwing my towel in the swimming pool sort of thing – but some of the people doing it were very funny, and, when they forgot to be arseholes, I enjoyed school. When they called me 'Ginga dog', or more usually just 'dog', it was less appealing.

Even if I were at school now, it would be hard to discern inattentive symptoms in someone also having absence seizures, or impulsive symptoms if they are simply young and immature. How do you tell if someone is being bullied because they are neurodiverse or, to borrow another nineties term, 'sad'? As we each have our constellation of ADHD symptoms, we have the tapestry of conditions, coincidences, joys and challenges that explain the person we have become – I have never quite forgiven one magazine editor for casually describing tall girls as alien in a newspaper column, for example. It is genuinely lovely to hear from friends and their kids how much better schools are now at helping children understand their emotions and develop empathy, especially those dorky little souls who need to be shepherded through social conventions with extra care.

All this meant I experienced depression, not learning what that was for years. I had trouble sleeping. At night, my brain would ping back on with thoughts about the house catching fire and my not being able to wake everyone, and wondering how much it would hurt to jump out of a first-floor window if I used a duvet to break my fall. I felt constantly awful, and by my late teens I self-harmed to get the feelings out of my body, if not my mind. I went to my GP in my first year of university when I was feeling suicidal – I had made a plan, but it was more to escape and to switch off the feelings than wanting death – and they gave me antidepressants and referred me to counselling. I managed one session before the counsellor blamed someone else for my problems, and I left in an indignant rage. I would try therapy again; but without knowing what the underlying problem was, there wasn't much I could truly achieve.

While not a medical comorbidity, simply keeping your life together can be one of the biggest obstacles to seeking a diagnosis. Although often well intentioned, the term 'high-functioning' is one of my most loathed as it suggests that as long as you're producing or not causing anybody any inconvenience, it's okay. Nobody aspires to be functional. A 'high-functioning' human being is basically a robot. I was falling apart under the surface, but I was careful to at least try and keep this fact from the world, however unsuccessfully.

NAOMI, 26: A lot of symptoms have been suppressed because, in certain communities, you just can't do things. In Nigerian culture, I can't speak back to my parents – that just doesn't run – so where I've been punished every time I do that, even though I may interrupt people naturally because I have ADHD, I've suppressed that part of me. It would manifest in a different way. I may not have been spotted as someone who has ADHD as fast as someone who's allowed to just exist in that way, you know. Even being creative and wanting to pursue that is not supported because of the way marginalised communities don't really have access to those kinds of jobs, so even there, I've had to force my brain to try and be more a certain type of way, whereas someone who may not have those constraints will then present differently. There's that huge gap of, okay, both people have ADHD, but one person may have had to figure out a way to just deal with it because it wasn't allowed to grow or flourish.

JO, 63: I couldn't understand why I struggled with so many things. I was misdiagnosed with general anxiety disorder, depression and OCD before I discovered that it was probably ADHD and was diagnosed at fifty-five. Five years later, I was diagnosed with autism.

MICHELLE, 41: About a month after my ADHD diagnosis, I got one for autism spectrum disorder. I hadn't thought much of it at the time, but when I'd completed my ADHD assessment, the lady said that there were things in there I might want to explore. I didn't understand the concept. You don't, because we don't really talk about it, right? A week later, I was on a bus scrolling through some Instagram posts from @AutisticCallum and @SpectrumGirl, and I was like, 'Oh, my dad does that all the time.' I've always thought my dad was just a grumpy person, and then I realised, 'Oh my God, my dad's autistic.' I went to the next post and almost burst into tears because I was like, 'Oh my God, I do that.' It was more of a shock that I was autistic than that I had ADHD, probably because I'd had more time to prepare for the ADHD. I'd been diagnosed with depression, anxiety and disordered eating in my teens. I also break myself quite a lot, so there is currently a suspicion I have EDS [Ehlers-Danlos syndrome]. On one visit to my osteopath, he said, 'You know, Michelle, I think you've displaced some ribs.' I've had the same pain on and off since I was twenty; I'd stop exercising for six months at a time, and now I know if I break myself, it's probably to do with this EDS. It's irritating, but thankfully, it's not serious enough to put my life in danger. I always just thought I was stressed. I didn't understand the concept of anxiety until my doctor described the symptoms. When you learn more about autism, there's something called alexithymia, which means you don't necessarily recognise your emotions, so to me, excitement and anxiety can often feel the same. I'm learning and navigating through all these interesting labels I now have, which is better than thinking, 'Oh my God, what's wrong with me?'

AL, 41: I started taking antidepressants when I went to university. I was diagnosed with emotionally unstable personality disorder. Then it was borderline personality disorder. Then it was bipolar two, so I had ten years of taking Lamotrigine, and then it was major depressive disorder. When an old friend was diagnosed with ADHD and started an Instagram account, I followed it to be supportive and realised, 'I don't like this. This is a bit confronting.' I muted it for a while, sat on it for a few months, then returned to it and thought, 'Okay, let's look at this properly.' I still have days where I'm convinced I don't have ADHD. When I told my dad, he said, 'You've had so many diagnoses; what's different about this one?' I struggled a bit when I was first diagnosed. I had a real period of grief about what it might have looked like had I been diagnosed earlier because I dropped out of university; I spent twelve weeks in rehab – it's been chaos. And we look back, and I go, 'Oh.' My dad found my Year Ten school reports, and every comment was just ADHD all over. Three of my best friends are GPs, and six are medics, and I feel a level of responsibility to try and help them understand – not for my own sake, but so that they can have more of an awareness when they're with their patients. I can't say it to everybody, but I want to be taken seriously by them. I don't want to think of people like me not being diagnosed until they're forty because they're going round the houses, or they don't want to talk to their GP about it, or their GP doesn't recognise the signs.

DANIELLE, 44: I'm a product of the Catholic education system, which is quite mainstream in Australia. My mum had tried to get me tested for dyslexia, but teachers kept saying, 'There's no way Danielle has a learning disability,' – which is what everybody here calls all of these things, by the way – 'she's not stupid. She's not dumb.' When I was eventually diagnosed with it in my thirties, I did a whole bunch of treatments that worked well, but I could never get the focus that helped with setting other techniques.

I'd also been diagnosed with arthritis during my first pregnancy and later with an autoimmune condition, so there was a lot going on, but once the ADHD got under control, the most amazing thing happened. Rather than being a frequent flyer at the GP's office, my health got better. I went from, 'I'm in pain all the time. My life sucks. I've got two small kids. I'm trying to pick them up, and this is really hard,' to, 'Oh shit! I can actually do this. I've got the energy that I need.' Once I was assessed and treated, I was able to eat better, and I stopped drinking. All that stuff was way easier to do in a world where my brain was more regulated. I'm just getting over COVID, but on a normal week, I exercise six days out of seven. Because I'm able to do that and the healthy eating, I've got lots more energy, and I can keep up with the kids a lot better. It's still hard, and my spoons aren't great, but I've gone from feeling I'm at breaking point every day to, 'We got to the end of today, and I do not feel like a broken wreck of a human being!'

ANDY, 52: I know I'm a mess, but I understand how my mess works. I try to go with it in a positive way. One of the reasons I get a bit wound up by all the pigeonholing that goes on is that just the term 'neurotypical' assumes that there is such a thing as a 'normal' person with a 'normal' way of thinking, and I don't buy that. The human brain is the most complex object in the known universe, and it comes in all sorts of shapes and sizes. If there's the bucket of neurodiversity, then inside that you've got all these little pigeonholes, but loads of them overlap because it's so messy and complex, then that's even more true of neurotypicals.

We now know that many of the symptoms of post-COVID syndrome or long COVID are almost indistinguishable from ADHD. Brain fog, distractibility, lack of focus, all the rest, it's like, 'Okay, welcome to the party, pal.' Then, during the early lockdowns, all the extroverts were going nuts. Now you know how us introverts feel at a party. That's what it's like for people who don't think like you; not everybody has to fit into your box. The lockdowns were stressful for everybody. It was a tough time – a global pandemic, and people died. It just goes to show how different people's experience of the world is – staying home and reading books and watching telly and digging around on the internet? I do that anyway; there's basically no change for me, but it's incredibly stressful for other people.

ANNABELLE, 51: I was diagnosed with ADHD, ASD and sensory processing disorder. It's a huge one for me; I hate bright lights and loud noises. I love clubs with techno music and strobing lights, but I hate the sunshine. I'm like a vampire, and everyone's like, 'What's wrong with you?' All these little things, every single thing I've wondered about myself, are answered to a certain degree.

HANNAH, 50: The most significant impact ADHD has had has been on my self-esteem, my feeling about who I am. It really affected me at school. I found it very difficult to retain information and wanted to do risky things instead of concentrating on schoolwork. I do wonder how different things might have been for me if I'd been diagnosed – and I'm much more ADHD, I'm only mildly dyslexic – I wish I'd had therapy or medication when I was younger. It's very hard, isn't it, going through life feeling that there's something wrong with you? Especially if you've got a parent who makes you feel shameful, who's not nurturing and caring and who's very critical of how you are and who you are. As a result, I made a self-fulfilling prophecy: 'If you're going to call me a slut, I might as well just go off and be one.' Not having that safe, secure nurturing and not being fully accepted and loved for who you are, for your strengths and weaknesses, was very difficult. To not feel accepted for who I was, for my worst qualities, being scatty and forgetful and bumping into things and saying the wrong thing or talking, you know, a million to the dozen. It was not okay to be like that.

PROFESSIONAL VIEW

DR SHYAMAL MASHRU: There's a two-hit hypothesis for most mental health conditions. The first hit is genetics; the second is environment. There is a theory that there is no such thing as ADHD and it is only trauma alone. I would not entirely agree with this. I believe ADHD exists as a biological condition and then the trauma experienced in the patient's life in childhood (due to their symptoms) exacerbates their symptoms and compensatory behaviours later on in life. It's not just a family history of ADHD, which is separate from a family history of bipolar – there's a spectrum that you're seeing. If you have the genetics for a mental health condition, you've had the first hit. It's a vulnerability you're born with that you can't do anything about.

The second hit is in the environment. Trauma is a big environmental factor. You're very likely to develop RSD [rejection sensitivity dysphoria] if your parents constantly criticised you because you couldn't do certain things. You're very likely to develop comorbid anxiety and depression if you don't have any support networks or a supportive employer or you never had supportive teachers and were always berated. It's human nature. What's going to happen? You're going to feel terrible, aren't you? I think people medicalise things too much. Just think about it; anyone would feel like that. You'll have poor self-esteem if you weren't told it's okay to be the way you are or if your parents never told you, 'We're proud of you, though. You're a good person.' What's your perception of yourself going to be? In terms of the messages given as a child, you could classify that as trauma, depending on how badly it was perceived. A bad experience is different to you than it is to me. Those are the big factors that shape someone and how they view themselves.

The emotional dysregulation in ADHD is not currently part of the diagnostic classification system, but I will be shocked if it's not in future. It's huge. Emotional dysregulation is when people get overwhelmed with their emotions. It might not look like that big a deal to the external person, so why are they overreacting? There's a reason for that as well. Because people have been criticised for their difficulties throughout their lives, it can produce intense emotional responses to specific situations, which can be very hard to manage and control. You've got to look at ADHD as not just a purely medical model and ask why that is happening in that person. Look at their life history closely, and if you interview enough people, you start seeing patterns because all these things are concerns that someone will be perceived in a certain way over bad experiences.

The research shows that 70 to 80 per cent of patients with ADHD have anxiety and low mood in their lifetime, and it makes sense. In my opinion, it's not the generalised anxiety disorder many people get diagnosed with, although some people do have that. Many patients I see with ADHD don't think in that catastrophic way about everything; it's more in certain situations. You get given a dissertation deadline, and it's a few months away. With time blindness and object impermanence, that disappears into the background until it hits you when it's due. Those kinds of task-related anxiety then cause overwhelming anxiety. From a human nature perspective, think about having that running theme throughout your life. You get told at school, 'Kat's got a lot of potential, but she doesn't apply herself. Kat's lazy.' Or even with well-meaning parents: 'Kat's untidy; why is her bedroom always so messy?' People often describe not meeting their potential in their careers. Eventually, you might start believing the rhetoric: 'Maybe I'm just not that good. Why is it such a struggle for me to achieve things compared to my colleagues? Why am I working until eight o'clock in the evening and she finished at four?' Over time, that will affect your self-esteem and lead to episodes of depression. People perceive rejection so intensely because of how they perceive themselves. That's why they become very sensitive about it; it's a protective mechanism, ego defence. People with RSD, higher-functioning people particularly, strive for perfectionism because they know that they've made careless mistakes throughout their lives, and so they need to check this email a hundred times before sending it out. There's a logical progression in the emotions; you can't just label it as RSD being ADHD. Well, why is RSD seen in ADHD? There's a process that's happening in someone's life here that makes them that way.

There is a group of patients with comorbid and separate clinical depression and anxiety, and those patients will describe doing well on typical SSRI antidepressants. But then you see a patient telling you, 'I've tried every antidepressant under the sun, and they haven't done anything for me, and they riddled me with side effects.' SSRI antidepressants are horrendous for side effects, in all honesty, especially trying to come off them, and people then mistake it as maybe it was working when that's the withdrawal effect. You've got to ask about ADHD when you see a patient who's giving you that history.

Consider ADHD and bipolar disorder. Taking a good clinical history is key because there are subtle differences. In bipolar disorder, you'll typically see episodes of weeks to months of low mood followed by weeks of hypomania [a less extreme form of mania]. The emotional dysregulation you see in ADHD is diurnal; it's happening throughout the day itself. That's not what's classically happening in bipolar. There is a very rare type of bipolar called rapid cycling bipolar where that can happen, but that's extremely rare, and very few true cases have ever been seen. But by and large, if you don't ask about timing if someone says I'm up and down with my moods, and then you stick them on a bloody mood stabiliser – it's the wrong medication, and now you've riddled someone with the side effects.

You can't just paint all mental health with one brush, but you need to be clear about what kind of emotional dysregulation is happening in ADHD; otherwise, you'll class it as something incorrect. I've seen so many patients in the clinic who've been on tons of different medications, including mild antipsychotics, to try to balance out their mood, and it's the wrong stuff. But suppose someone has genuine bipolar disorder and ADHD symptoms, and they're not treated for their bipolar disorder with a mood stabiliser. In that case, if you give them a stimulant, they're at ten times increased risk of developing mania. If someone has genuine psychotic symptoms or mild grade, and you give them a stimulant, they will be fully blown psychotic. It's not an easy process.

PROFESSOR PHILIP ASHERSON: A secondary care mental health services study found that around 20 per cent of people with ADHD had another diagnosis. The rate of missed ADHD in the population might be 2 or 3 per cent overall, but if you take a group with an ongoing mental health problem, it will be much higher. I've never seen a thorough primary care study of patients with chronic anxiety and depression, yet there will be a lot of undiagnosed ADHD in that group.

If you don't know what ADHD is, the symptoms could look like another condition: anxiety and depression, for example, because people worry about their problems, have low self-esteem and present with depressive symptoms. Emotional dysregulation is also widespread, although by no means specific to ADHD. Many aspects are shared across mental health, so if you look superficially at an irritable person with low self-esteem who can't sleep, you think, 'Oh, it could be anxiety or depression.' Then ADHD was never on that list of things to think about.

You need to know what you're looking for and what is specifically ADHD. Depression, for example, clearly isn't one thing. It can be normal grief, it can be a reaction to something in your life, or it could be a severe episodic condition. Many people with ADHD can dip in and out of low moods and develop chronic low self-esteem and feelings of poor self-worth, which over time is akin to a kind of depression, but it's knowing that there is a primary reason behind it. With some symptoms, it's better to think of them more like having a fever. Then you've got to say, 'Okay, well, what's causing the fever?' ADHD is more like an underpinning cause of all sorts of different problems.

Some areas of psychiatry need to be better understood or characterised, but the core understanding of ADHD is not the problem; it's a matter of expertise, experience and explanation. There is enough information and data to say this is what it is and how it differs from other conditions. People need to understand that it's not like an episode of anxiety and depression. They tend to come and go, whereas ADHD is something to manage every day of your life. It doesn't go away because it's a characteristic of you. It's rather unusual. People debate whether it is a mental health disorder or a neurodiversity. Some people don't want to say it's a mental health issue, but clearly, it causes mental health problems, and there are medical treatments, so it is a mental health issue in that sense. But then, many people don't necessarily feel mentally unwell. Many people with ADHD seem to thrive and don't want to think that they have a condition, so they're much happier with maybe thinking of themselves as being neurodiverse.

DR ELLIE DOMMETT is a reader in neuroscience and Deputy Director of undergraduate psychology at King's College London, where she also leads the ADHD Research Lab (@ADHDResearchLab), conducting studies with a particular focus on adults.

We do struggle with getting males into trials. I don't know if they're not interested in taking part in studies or if they don't have the organisational skills, but I've been turning down women for the last month and a half. If I take more, I'll have to change all the analysis; it'll be a study about women. I've got to have both, or it doesn't work. A problem with a lot of research is that to make good science, you have to control everything. ADHD is such an umbrella of symptoms that it's impossible to find 'perfect' people to participate in a trial because they won't have the same symptoms. We did include anxiety and depression if they weren't medicated, but that was partly to ensure we wouldn't ask people to exercise when they perhaps have a medication that could alter their blood pressure. For our adolescent trial, we will include as many co-occurring conditions as possible whilst not mucking up our ability to do any statistics, so not having something that might mean someone can't exercise but things like oppositional defiant disorder and conduct disorder don't make any difference to their ability to exercise.

It's interesting from a history of psychiatry perspective. Take psychosis as an example. Some people would say psychosis is one umbrella term for conditions such as schizophrenia, bipolar disorder, etc. In contrast, others say not to define those conditions and to say psychosis in general. But suppose somebody presents with 'psychosis', and you put them on lithium. If they have schizophrenia, that drug won't make any difference, so there's a good reason to separate it out. It's a bit like how we can recognise 'neurodiversity' or separate that into ADHD, autism, dyslexia and Tourette's. A case can be made for both approaches.

PROFESSOR SUSAN YOUNG: It was only recognised in 2013 that you could have ADHD and ASD comorbidly. That was with pressure from scientific journals consistently finding genetic and clinical overlap. Until then, for anyone working in ADHD services, the differential diagnosis would be ASD: you have to decide which it is. Then vice versa in ASD services: you'd have to rule out ADHD, so you'd have to know a lot about the other. Now they're comorbid you have to consider in greater detail whether the person has had this at a level of disorder or not. You have to do less to rule it out if you like than to rule it in. Within the genetic profile of the different developmental conditions, there is an overlap, which makes sense when you do an ADHD assessment and see people with sensory processing difficulties.

Then I have to ask, do they have ADHD and autism – a full diagnosis? Often, they don't; they have ADHD with some symptoms of autism, which fall sub-threshold to clinical disorder. Or vice versa: you get people with autism who present very much with an inattentive, impulsive profile, but it's sub-threshold to having the whole ADHD. My daughter has ADHD, and when she was little, she would walk on her toes like a ballerina. It wasn't till later that I discovered that's something people with autism do.

CHAPTER FOUR

Treatment

The happy-ever-after joy I got from my diagnosis lasted approximately three days before the red velvet curtain went up again, and reality set in. Perhaps I could blame Disney for my addiction to happy-ever-afters. I went into marriage with my eyes wide open, but there were many elements of life where it simply did not occur to me what might happen after a Big Successful Moment. When I won a journalism award, I was genuinely surprised that nobody approached me afterwards to commission me to write a column or review a hotel. When I ran the London Marathon during my running obsession, I was so shocked by how mundane it felt to cross the finish line that my brain went into meltdown. I had imagined something like a chorus singing my name, not my having to continue to put one foot in front of the other. Instead of having my photograph taken to celebrate my conversion from couch potato to athlete, I was taken away by the St John Ambulance, who laid me on a sofa and took off my trainers while I hyperventilated.

I had imagined that, post-diagnosis, I might instinctively know how to manage life like a video-game character unlocking a new move. It occurred to me that this was a pause, not a conclusion. On an everyday basis, nothing had changed. I hadn't magically become consistent. I didn't drink alcohol any more, but I still guzzled coffee and sugar like a trash panda, and I would regularly get to five in the afternoon and have to go to bed because I couldn't function.

Money was also an issue. When I'd locked on to private diagnosis, I hadn't thought through what would happen next as regards ongoing costs. The timing wasn't great for a hefty consultation charge with medication on top, in a pandemic when my work had dried up, and I was doing the vaccine trial at my local hospital to scoop up forty-five quid every month or so – splendid. Yes, I would eventually be able to go into a shared care agreement between my psychiatrist and the NHS, and so have the cost lowered to NHS rates, but only once I was stable on meds. Even then, I would need a six-monthly review at two hundred quid a pop. Well, if it isn't the consequences of my own actions.

Someone asked me if I was ever tempted to buy Ritalin and move on without a diagnosis or prescription, and while I was waiting for my assessment, a friend gave me some of their instant-release medication to try, mainly to see if it would help. I couldn't rely on that in the longer term, nor did I want to. I wanted answers and to go through this with a doctor, not least to get the right meds.

I was also quite desperate to be treated with stimulant medication. I'd heard so much about how they nipped binge eating in the bud, got your brain focusing again, and generally seemed to work miracles. I wanted mine! I was almost a year sober when I was diagnosed, but because I had a history of problem drinking, I needed several tests before being prescribed stimulants: blood tests, an ECG, and so on. I was able to have these done through the NHS, but due to my GP losing the results in the chaos of the pandemic, it was three months after diagnosis before I started meds.

Unfortunately, my first trial of stimulants didn't agree with me – the irony, after all those sodding tests. I was distraught. During times of stress or, more realistically, every day, I tend towards all-or-nothing thinking. With stimulants, I'd latched on to the idea that something would fix me, and when they didn't, I lost it. Sulkily, I agreed to try non-stimulants while fixating on going onto stimulant meds again 'when these didn't work'. They did work, which was annoying. It wasn't an instant fix by any stretch of the imagination, but they did the job. Over the next year, my meds were tweaked a few times and have been again more recently, which is also why I wanted to do this with a doctor. You can change something if it doesn't work or if you don't like it. ADHD meds have been rigorously researched because they're used on children, but it doesn't mean it won't take a while to find the right regimen. I was offered a DNA test to see what meds I might best respond to, but even my spendthrift brain drew the line at a grand, so trial and error it was. As other life stuff has happened, so has my medication changed – I've gone from only taking the non-stimulant atomoxetine to including Elvanse in the afternoon and dexamfetamine in the morning to combat fatigue, along with an antidepressant and a beta blocker for anxiety. Sometimes, I take them all, sometimes not – the stimulants are out of your system by the end of the day, whereas the non-stimulants last longer. Treating ADHD is not one-and-done, not even in terms of treatment, and it is specific to everyone.

My hobbies dwindled as I prioritised paying for medication and therapy for ADHD and then for my left hip, which was becoming aggressively painful and which I was waiting to have replaced. This complication meant I couldn't do much of the exercise I used to blow off steam, which sent me further into my head. While medication is incredibly effective for ADHD, it is not the only part of treatment. General therapy is essential for understanding your identity and life so far. Processing what has happened helps to understand yourself and can shed new light on memories full of shame, regret and guilt and transform them into something quieter, more peaceful and more self-accepting.

Also essential, if less immediately clear how to access, is behavioural therapy or coaching. As adults, we may have made up for our brain's quirks with fairly questionable coping strategies. When medication is under way, therapy – through talking, exercise and meditation – is needed to help unpick habits that are now learned behaviours because moving past them is real work. Privately, at least, therapy is more straightforward – go to the BCPA website, find a qualified therapist whose experience and specialisms look right and give them a go. Going through the NHS is significantly more challenging due to the demand and lack of resources. Coaching is more of a challenge. The recommendations I have had have come through my therapist and through the government's Access to Work scheme (more of which later) – until I started those sessions, my coaching came from books, podcasts, Instagram and YouTube.

Once I was medicated, there was no need for me to consume the sugary treats and buckets of coffee I used to coax my brain into action, yet I kept on doing both. Treats had become a habit as much as putting clean underwear on each morning. Treats made me feel looked after. They were the carrot I used after the stick of how I 'should' do better, work harder and generally be a completely different person. Therapy and coaching helped me to identify areas like these that weren't serving me any more – and to find other things that might bring me pleasure and uplift if and when I can free my vice-like grip on children's birthday-party food. It also gave me a place to talk through other things that were going on for me that were impacted by the ADHD, like the distress I felt at not being able to escape my thoughts as I got increasingly depressed around my hip replacement operation. There's a line from *Hamlet*, embedded in my brain since school: 'When sorrows come, they come not single spies, but in battalions.' It could have been written about ADHD, let alone the everyday challenges of living. Knowing this doesn't make it any easier to accept, which is why we need this three-pronged approach of therapy, coaching and meds – even if implementing it all, alongside exercise and lifestyle adjustments like decent food and sleep hygiene, can feel like more hills to climb. When I have the energy to do that, I'm all in. When I don't – well, rewatching my favourite seasons of *Bake Off* does some pretty heavy lifting.

What has been your experience of treatment?

SEAN, 38: I was sent straight to a psychiatrist – there was no mention of therapy. The guy was lovely and supportive. The first chat we had was about two hours. And then he said, 'Right, we'll try you on Xaggitin XL,' an extended-release stimulant that has worked really well. Beyond that, there's been no support. I had follow-ups with the same psychiatrist, but it was really strange: he's gone from this understanding guy who was great to talk to, and so validating to, 'Okay, so has medication solved these ten things?' Well, no, because I'm unlearning thirty-five years of habits. There were three or four follow-ups, and they were all, 'That sounds like the drugs are working, off you go.' So, beyond that, it's just been support from people I know with ADHD, talking things through with them and hearing about coping strategies they've developed. There's been no sort of official support. The other trap you can fall into once Instagram figures out that you've got ADHD is that it's all over adverts or on your Explore page: all these accounts that are like, 'Hey! Does this sound like you? Buy my book or sign up for our courses,' which I have mixed feelings about. On the one hand, they probably are just trying to help and make a living at the same time, which is fair enough. But you start to feel a computer's figured out you've got ADHD, and now you're being targeted, which I find really creepy.

JAMES, 47: I know medication has helped a lot of people, but I feel like I've dealt with it so far; I've lived this long and learned to adapt to it so I don't really think I want to medicate for it. I imagine medication could be quite life-changing, but I'm still a bit reluctant. Instead, I've had tons of therapy. Weirdly, I found the therapist quite unhelpful in an ADHD capacity because I just don't think they know enough about it. They understand it in broad terms, but they're not experts. And also, I know my brain. Therapy has given me a lot of self-awareness and understanding of how my brain works on a basic level, and understanding how ADHD works means I understand my brain in a way that I didn't before so I can compensate for things. Sometimes, I can't do anything about it; awareness doesn't always give you a solution. I know this is about my brain, but I don't necessarily have a way to get out of that situation because it is what it is. But I think knowing at least helps.

EMILY, 48: At my daughter's first appointment about ADHD meds, she told the psychiatrist, 'I've one best friend, and that's all I need.' She'd never go up for anything at school, just too anxious about everything, and then she started on the meds and, within six months, she's ended up with this massive mixed-gender friendship group. They did a big Shakespeare Festival with the school; she did a poetry competition; she signed up for the Duke of Edinburgh scheme – these things that she just never wanted to do, and suddenly, her world just blossomed. She still has anxiety and a meltdown if she thinks she will get in trouble at school; she always wants to be very good, which we're working on. I'm like, please be a little bit bad. But generally, watching her engage with other people in her life is amazing, and I am convinced it's the knowing more than the meds. Yes, the meds are amazing, and yes, they help her study and her brain be more functional, but the key is understanding why you feel different. Sometimes, she'll have a tantrum, and afterwards she'll say, 'I think that was my RSD; I was just being really sensitive, and I'm sorry.' It's great that she has that self-awareness at thirteen, which I'm just acquiring now. I was pro-medication pretty much right away. There's something that's going to make me feel better? Fine! If I have to take them for the rest of my life, like the meds I take for PTSD, like I would take insulin, I don't care. I'm not fussy or funny about those things. If there's a drug that'll make me work differently, then let's do it. But at the same time, because I can choose to take it or not, what don't I know yet? You can't know what you don't know. I'm constantly craving information but also careful about sifting it, like I've got a giant cheesecloth I'm trying to drape over the world. And yes, TikTok is great, but it's hardly a licensed practitioner. I don't have to have all my information from psychiatrists or medical professionals, but I have to know the information I'm getting is useful. If not, why am I bringing it into my life?

LAURA, 38: I wish I'd taken medication sooner, without a doubt. I understand why my mom wanted me to wait because, if you're a parent, giving your twelve-year-old amphetamines is probably a pretty tricky thing to ratify. Still, if I had been on it even two years earlier, I think

I would have had a much easier time in line with when school starts to get academically challenging and mean something to your future. It's scary how young that pressure starts. I wish that the penny had dropped for my mom earlier, but that's just the way it was at the time.

There's this real internet steer away from having a conversation about medication versus not having medication because, presumably, people don't want to be seen to be pushing what are essentially amphetamines. Very few people have had the chance to do what I've done in that they've had their school days on it and then, as an adult, taken a decision to have a break. I went to film school still taking Adderall because my dad had permission from a neurologist in the States to bring medication over to the UK for me. When my dad retired, we lost that supply, and there was nothing similar. I tried Dexedrine and it was dreadful; it just gave me a headache. The idea of hyperfocus, when it's something your brain is really locked into and that you find interesting and engaging, meant work wasn't difficult to stick with, so during my first ten years in the industry, I didn't take medication at all.

What pushed me back to looking into it was a course where I spent two days sitting there being talked at, which is my brain's worst nightmare. I was using every ounce of me to try and make sure that I was paying attention, then getting to the end of the day and feeling exhausted. It was like my brain desperately needed to shut off and escape from focusing on anything. There were other things, too:

my husband had been talking to me about when I first met one of his friends who we work with, and he was laughing about it, just saying, 'She thought you didn't like her when we first met because you blanked her all the time.' And I'm like, shit, is this something I'm doing at work? This is worse than not just being able to pay attention. I will also cut people off, which is a classic ADHD trait. I can't focus on conversations with five people so my brain shuts off. I lose interest instantly, so I'll blank people. Then I'll come back in, and I might talk over someone.

Deciding to take meds again turned out to be interesting timing because about three years prior, Elvanse had been introduced to the UK market, and it has a very similar chemical composition to Adderall. I have a pretty encyclopaedic knowledge of brands and ADHD drugs, so I tried that and realised what I'd been missing and hadn't been doing. It was like turning a light on in my brain. Everything felt effortless in that way that people who don't have ADHD don't understand. It's not just that you can't focus; getting through a small to-do list can feel like Everest. Maybe that's what people with normal brain chemistry can't understand – 'Why on earth is it so hard for you to get this done?' It just is. It's like wrestling with a squirrel in your brain. You catch it for two seconds, and then oh no, it's off again. Getting the squirrel to sit still is exhausting; trying to catch it is exhausting. Take medication, and suddenly, there's no squirrel at all.

In the States, you have slow-release Adderall, which lasts the whole day and releases into your system at an even rate, whereas Elvanse is like a fucking baseball bat: bam, there it is in your system. Then, it'll wear off towards the end of the day because it doesn't release slowly. I hope that more understanding helps the UK market to release something better. It's crazy to me that we can't get Adderall here. It's just a much more elegant drug – which sounds like a weird thing to say, but it has a better sustain. There's no way I could take Elvanse all the time. It's too punchy in the morning and not enough later in the day. I know you can do things like take a bit and then top it up, but I can't be bothered to start splitting open pills and trying to measure things out, and that wouldn't suit me at work.

I give myself medication breaks. I don't take it on the weekend or if I'm not working unless there's a good reason. If you don't have loads of stuff to do, it's nice to mentally slow down because you can't always stay up at this level. Like it or not, when it's a pain in the ass to live with, it is your body's natural brain chemistry, and you're still having to feed yourself a pretty powerful cocktail of drugs to bring it up to what society has conceived as the level you should run at. Sometimes, I don't want always to feel completely focused. Sometimes, I quite like my brain as it is. My brain's a pretty relaxed place when I'm not on it. If you're trying to unwind, it's nice not to take it.

PROFESSIONAL VIEW

DR SHYAMAL MASHRU: Patients tell me, 'I don't want to be on a stimulant, my brain feels overstimulated as it is.' If you look at it from a medical perspective, the brain in ADHD is in a state of chronic understimulation or quick to boredom, and that's where I look at the term 'stimulant', so it's not the way we'd usually look at it in English. Stimulants are primarily designed to increase your dopamine and noradrenaline levels, particularly in the brain's frontal area. There are two chemical types: methylphenidate and amphetamine-based stimulants. Methylphenidates primarily work by blocking the reuptake of dopamine and noradrenaline. Amphetamine-based stimulants will block the reuptake of dopamine and noradrenaline and increase production. But overall, both will have the same effect of increasing those two neurotransmitters at the level of the brain, which is a very simplified way of looking at this. Interestingly, the research shows there might be other chemicals involved in ADHD as well.

Non-stimulants, such as atomoxetine and guanfacine, work by increasing noradrenaline levels. Stimulants and non-stimulants work in slightly different ways, primarily regarding rates of action. Stimulants work quickly. That's why, within a month or two, people will say, 'It's transformed me.' Non-stimulants work slowly, a bit more like antidepressants, and take up to six months to take full effect.

There's some evidence base behind using things like guanfacine, which is a non-stimulant, to treat symptoms of RSD. And that's used alongside the stimulant, so you're putting people on both. Certain non-stimulants like guanfacine were initially used to treat blood pressure. It was never designed for this. It just showed that it seems to have these effects, and it came from children because on the NHS, guanfacine is prescribed to kids with ADHD, but it's not licensed in adults on the NHS. Certainly, in the US and Canada, where I feel they're more advanced with their ADHD treatments, people often use stimulant and non-stimulant medications.

One thing I've realised is that like any chronic condition, even physical health conditions, treatment is a mixture of chemistry and environment. Massively, actually. There has to be a chemical underpinning going on here. Otherwise, medication wouldn't do diddly squat, right? Medication is very effective, but it's definitely not the only answer. When I started this work, I thought, 'Oh, just take the stimulants; that's what you do.' It's not enough. Lifestyle factors, ADHD coaching and general therapy come into play in a big way.

PROFESSOR PHILIP ASHERSON: The gold standard of treatment would be a combination of medication – if you need it and it works for you – and coaching from an expert who understands ADHD and can help you learn how to manage it better. Even people on medication will experience symptoms. Sometimes, it's a miracle cure, but more often, it's controlling something and helping you, but it doesn't necessarily just take it all away. Some problems have developed over time, and people need a lot of help to unlearn and learn new ways of being. Of course, many people may not want or don't need medication if their ADHD is mild enough or they function well in other aspects of their lives, and they may be quite determined to find ways of helping themselves.

The ideal would be treatment through an NHS service. There are many private services, but it is not always easy to know who's good and who isn't. Linking up with an ADHD support group might be very helpful because they could give you their perspective on who's helped and hasn't helped them – AADD-UK, for example, or ADDISS. There are excellent ADHD coaches out there, but it's not a regulated profession, so you really don't know other than by word of mouth. That's a problem shared with psychotherapy and other areas. The fact that anybody can do it is problematic.

Cheatsheet: How to eat when stimulant medication steals your appetite

Vitamin C: Avoid juice, fruit or supplements for an hour before and after you take meds, as it can stop them from being absorbed.

Protein powder: A handy no-think breakfast or other meal when you're 'on'. Bulk is a British brand that produces grass-fed whey and vegan powders – the chocolate mint one is very good, and their packaging is largely sustainable. You need to blend it, or it's just undrinkable powdery water, but that has wildly improved the cost per wear of the Nutribullet I was briefly obsessed with in 2015.

Nuts and seeds: An area where you should absolutely embrace the ADHD squirrel stereotype. Get as wide a variety as possible: almonds, walnuts, Brazil nuts, pecans and pistachios; flaxseed, pumpkin and chia are all great for extra fibre, protein and omega-3s. Protein gets all the press, but the fibre is vital for keeping you full and nannying your innards when you've accidentally inhaled the supermarket.

Use your freezer: Keep bread for the toaster, peas, pre-chopped onion, bags of berries and anything that would otherwise go off and that you can chuck into something else without having to prep it first.

Lunch: This can be especially hard to bother with when you're in full flow. Have some no-thinking-required meals you can make quickly, then nibble on them as and when you remember through the afternoon. These are three of my go-tos.

- Beans on toast. Lots of protein, lots of fibre.
- Halved pepper with sliced avocado and lemon juice, eaten in my hands like a philistine sandwich.
- Yoghurt, freezer berries, nuts, seeds and cacao nibs for texture (yes, I know, thank you, just call me Heston Blumenthal).

CHAPTER FIVE

Exercise and lifestyle

In 2012, the headteacher of a Scottish primary school introduced fifteen minutes to the school day where children ran, jogged and wheeled. Elaine Wyllie's brainwave improved her pupils' physical health, but teachers reported that their classes were also calmer, happier, more alert and focused. In the years since, The Daily Mile has expanded to cover two million children in the UK and two million more worldwide.

Wyllie's genius was to remove all barriers to entry. She chose fifteen minutes because it's manageable for everyone and wasn't intensive enough to require a change of clothes. Finding something that works is the secret to exercise, and certainly, any that I have stuck to has been through a sense of purpose, ease or enjoyment. It was a shock when I became focused on running in my late twenties. My brother was the athlete; he used to run or cycle to work while I proceeded to the bus stop at a sedate amble. Then there I was, going on ten-mile runs on the weekend. How? What? Who was this person, and where had the previous incarnation gone?

My longstanding hatred of running came from school, where it was doled out through cross-country, sports day or the bleep test, and was based on distance or achievement rather than enjoyment. Exercise felt like a competition that others could do, and I could not. The closest I came to team sports was youth theatre. What I was missing was a reason why. Any old pillock could go for a walk around a field, but why would you bother when you could see it from horseback, bus or car, and so have someone do the walking for you?

London 2012 gave me my why. A summer of endorphins relentlessly pumped into the British public did more for exercise propaganda than any number of public health suggestions. The secret to exercising was joy. First, I spent months rehearsing for the Opening Ceremony as a drummer, walking in step around the old Ford car factory in East Ham; then there was the night itself, seeing a sudden, thrilled understanding break across the faces of the crowd. I haunted the reselling website and got tickets for synchronised swimming and Para-dressage to see it all up close. I usually found dressage the dullest of equestrian sports – I didn't have the patience to learn how to do it, let alone appreciate it – but watching Team GB's multi-medallist Lee Pearson riding his equally famous horse, Gentleman, so beautifully at Greenwich reignited a deep love that I'd had since I first inhaled my family's old pony books. The sweet, bosky scent of working horse unlocked childhood memories of greenery, speed and connection. I googled riding stables as soon as I got home and started out walking the hour to Dulwich from my Camberwell flat to ride at the little stables there, then getting the Tube up to more extensive stables in north London, then further and further out as my confidence and ability improved, and I made friends to go on riding adventures with outside the M25.

I kept up my lessons to improve and learn more, but I noticed a gap between my enjoyment of it and what happened when I was doing it. Once in the saddle, I had episodes that varied from mild anxiety to full-on terror, as though all the stress I experienced in day-to-day life burst out of the bottle when I was riding. 'It's supposed to be fun,' my poor instructor told me as I spent another lesson in tears. I found a hypnotherapist who specialised in riders to see if that would help. I tried an equine practitioner in emotional freedom technique, or tapping, who took me through any particular worries I held on to. I was so worried about what could happen that it became a case of a flight animal riding a flight animal. As years passed and I became more confident through simple repetition, the episodes lessened, but I couldn't understand what the hell the problem was. It didn't happen to anyone else. I started saying the serenity prayer before I rode to try to keep myself calm.

It was mystifying – I wasn't scared of it, but body and mind seemed to be disconnected, and it all started to make sense when I got my diagnosis.

After the olympics, I read Alexandra Heminsley's fantastic memoir *Running Like a Girl*, which healed all the scalding thoughts I had carried about running since school. The *Zombies, Run!* app took me the rest of the way by gamifying running until I loved it. I was so thrilled by doing something that I thought I couldn't do for so long that a picture of me grinning through the Royal Parks Half Marathon for Mind was put on their poster to lure in new fundraisers. The crucial thing was that I didn't compete, and, like riding, it became a part of my identity. I went to a running club once before realising I couldn't keep up, so I returned to solo runs around south London and merrily banging out 'Hail Holy Queen' from *Sister Act* when I needed a lift. This was for me, nobody else.

It all went tits up when I got carried away and signed up to the London Marathon. What had felt so wonderful, so moving to watch as a spectator, became overwhelming as a participant. This individual goal that was so precious, so unbelievable to me, soon became a vicarious outing for other people, usually sitting in deckchairs. Spectators, seeing my printed top, yelled, 'Come on, Kat,' in the bored tones of Brits who categorically cannot do encouragement. I was tweeting my way round to raise more money when a woman called, 'You'd go a lot faster if you got off your phone.' There were so many people to please and other runners and reminders of their time goals. Unlike my training races, a swathe of the London Marathon takes you through some of the dullest areas of the city, which killed my motivation. I didn't run again for two years. Whatever force was powering me through my running craze disappeared, and I couldn't get it back. I was gutted, so I leaned more into riding, while feeling incredibly guilty that I wasn't running or doing anything else to help myself become stronger. I kept trying to do yoga but always felt embarrassed that my hips refused to acknowledge the floor and I couldn't touch my toes. I now realise that I absolutely cannot do exercise that I'm not interested in but feel I 'should' do.

The summer that Pokémon Go became everyone's obsession was glorious. As my friends got into it, we all walked for miles. It made walking even around familiar places more exciting. I joined local raiding groups, where highly organised gangs of otherwise professional, grown-up adults would meet to take down bosses en masse. I played it while walking around Brisbane, using the city-wide Wi-Fi to catch Australian-specific Pokémon. I was really into it – really into it – and then suddenly lost interest and never touched it again. Luckily, I still had horse riding. There was enough variety in what could be done and where you could go. I could hire horses with friends and enjoy organised fun rides in beautiful locations around the country. I was riding consistently and regularly enough that I was improving as well as enjoying it. Unfortunately, the bilateral hip dysplasia that had seen my mother and aunt have hip replacements was now flaring up in me. My left hip was becoming sufficiently worn down as to dislocate at random intervals while walking. I stopped feeling at ease in the saddle and became more insecure. My stirrups never felt level simply because my legs were uneven.

As I've already mentioned, that routine operation became a grisly follow-up with two weeks in the hospital. I was out of my tree on antibiotics. I didn't do a stitch of physio. I knew I 'should'; I simply could not bring myself to do it. People I had met through riding, in person and on Instagram, kindly sent cards. Being unable to ride with them made me feel like my world was shrinking. I didn't realise how much I relied on it until I couldn't do it. The physical recovery from the operations was relatively fine, but the mental impact was alarming. I couldn't bring myself to look at my scar. My body felt separate in a way it hadn't done since I was zoning out through binge eating.

As the infection months wore on, my brain was trapped with no outlet. It ping-ponged relentlessly around the things I didn't have. I could deal with not drinking, I could deal with childlessness, with ADHD, but I needed riding to process everything in a more ritualistic and escapist way than I could achieve through therapy. That connection with a horse, that feeling that together you are one, the long rides through ravishing countryside, the percussive thrum of gallop, the sense of ecstatic flight when we jumped; all that made me feel utterly right with the world. It was so much more than exercise; it was magic, and old magic at that, connecting me to nature, community and beauty.

Everyone should have something where they feel that magic. Losing it is horrendous. My first step to coming back to it was through a friend from Instagram who incredibly generously let me ride her horse, Tony Hadley, a gorgeously named ex-showjumper. Emma had rehabbed him to health from the brink of being put down, and their yard was full of kindness. I was as delighted to play him Spandau songs to see which he enjoyed most as I was when we tried a few steps of canter through the woods. The anxiety that used to flood out when I was on horseback flowed into the ground because I now understood where it came from. With medication and understanding, I have more of the sensible level of caution that anyone about to ride should have, but it isn't the uncontrolled explosion it has been for so long. I am getting stronger, not just from working on my hip, but through chucking out what I 'should' be able to do if I were someone else, and leaning into what my brain accepts. I made my peace with needing somebody to come and make me do stuff, so I began to meet a lovely trainer in the park to do strength exercises while gossiping and admiring the trees. It's okay. It's the way it has to be, and in a few years, it will doubtless look completely different.

SEAN, 38: I was reading something about ADHD and exercise, which said we function best when we make it our entire personality. It probably won't stick for ever, but it will for a bit. It reminded me of a friend who was diagnosed last year. She had a long phase of running; she was doing marathons, and then she suddenly stopped, and I never really understood why. Now we know it's because she has ADHD, and that was just her obsession for a bit. She moved on to yoga, and then it was something else.

I've decided to get back into cycling. My dad is obsessed with it. He gave me a bike that he'd cobbled together a few years ago, which weirdly put me off. But finally, I'm like, no, I need to do something, I need to move. The bike needed work because it's been sitting outside for three years, so I put a new saddle on it and replaced the handlebar grips. I was ordering a new gear cable when I realised I was doing everything around this bike apart from fucking sitting on it. But I recognised that was a different feeling. It wasn't that I was not going to do this because there was no pressure but because I haven't ridden a bike for eight years, and I was scared about going outside the house and falling on my arse in front of the neighbours or crashing into a car. I had to shut up and try this and accept that I might fail, and I was able to push through that because I could recognise I knew this wasn't an ADHD thing. This is just nerves. I'm just anxious. This isn't not being able to phone the GP; this is what normal people experience when they don't want to do stuff, and I can deal with it. It's just recognising that difference between the ADHD wall and something difficult because of perfectly 'normal' reasons.

MICHELLE, 41: I love salsa dancing, but because you can just blow on my ankles and they'll roll, I can't do it – part of the challenges of EDS. I loved pole fitness in my early twenties, but I was never that good at it because I'd break myself one week and then be out for six. I discovered weightlifting, and I loved it – give me a deadlift any day of the week, and I'm a super happy bunny – but things like pole kept niggling at me. I went down a rabbit hole and trained as a nutrition coach; I did the Joe Wicks Body Coach thing. And it worked for a while. But every time, I returned to the fact that I couldn't do the stuff I enjoyed.

When someone mentioned flying trapeze, I went to a taster day, and I was hooked from the off. I've been doing that for seven years now. I've met amazing people who I class as friends as opposed to acquaintances. I could happily stay in my house for two weeks if I feel overwhelmed, but this gets me out. I need routine, and being able to book something in advance, knowing that I have to be there at a particular time, stops me from hyperfocusing on work because I love my job, and I could continue to 1 a.m.

And yes, I'm scared of heights, but jumping off the trapeze is the most exhilarating feeling in the world. Throwing yourself off a giant platform doesn't seem intuitive on that basis, but I get the biggest rush. I started aerial hoop in September because I needed a winter thing when the trapeze finishes for the summer. Between the two, it gives me something where my brain goes quiet. My ADHD is this constant hum of musical stuff, but if you're at the top of a trapeze platform, you're only thinking about the net and that you have to jump and get that bar. If you're upside down in a hoop, all you're thinking is, 'For God's sake, Michelle, hold on, or you're falling on your head.' It stops me from thinking so much, produces the dopamine I've needed for so long, and gives me a good night's sleep, which is challenging at the best of times.

THE PROFESSIONAL VIEW

DR SHYAMAL MASHRU: The research shows that regular physical exercise has a massive impact on ADHD symptoms. Huge. Not like anything ever seen in any other mental health condition. Stimulant medication targets low dopamine and noradrenaline levels in the brain, and during exercise, noradrenaline breaks down into adrenalin. Your body pumps out loads of adrenalin to make your heart beat and your muscles active, so you're increasing those levels by yourself – this also happens in fight-or-flight situations, which is also why people with ADHD almost require the threat of a dead-line to get their stuff done.

It also increases your dopamine levels. Even if you don't have ADHD, people always say that they feel much better when they exercise. Dopamine is one of the 'happy' hormones; it gets released during pleasure activities like sex, eating chocolate, or whatever does it for you. Taking drugs, for some people. Exercise is a healthy one and releases lots of those endorphins. Even if you don't have ADHD, this is what's happening in the body, but if you do have it, and those levels are low, that will have a big impact, and not just in terms of traditional symptoms. People with ADHD who exercise regularly will feel the emotional benefits far more than someone who doesn't have ADHD.

DR ELLIE DOMMETT: Originally, I researched drug addiction. Then, I stayed with the same drugs, amphetamine and methylphenidate, but started to look at their therapeutic use. I realised these drugs are fine and work quite well for some people, but some can't take them for medical reasons, and some don't want to. I'm looking at this as an outsider, but even as somebody who doesn't have ADHD and doesn't have children, I was aware of this worry from quite early on. I wasn't sure how I'd feel about giving my theoretical five-year-old amphetamine. Then I thought, 'If I had a five-year-old who was really struggling, I might change my mind.' I also realised that there were probably quite a lot of other things that would work.

When you look at the mechanisms of the drugs in the brain, there are other natural things that can do that, and of course, exercise is one, but the NICE guidelines on ADHD are pretty vague. 'Consider adjusting exercise.' Does that mean going for a walk or training for an ultra-marathon? When I looked more closely, it was clear that it focused on aerobic exercise. From a common-sense perspective, if you've got someone who may be hyperactive, you could argue that you're channelling that into exercise, or you could say, are we going to make it worse because you're encouraging them to run around for fitness purposes, so what about more calming forms of exercise like yoga?

We asked people with ADHD to tell us how they got to whatever point they were at with their exercise. Pre- and post-diagnosis, people recognised that they were exercising to manage their symptoms. Pre, they just found it made life a bit easier. And post, they contextualise that it's helping with their ADHD. But we found this all-or-nothing approach in that they got really into it, did loads and loads, got bored, stopped and did nothing. We came up with three themes: using exercise to manage ADHD and overtly knowing they were doing that; this roller coaster of going all in and then dropping out; and the third was around goals and structure, like training for a race or doing a particular activity and the idea that no one could take that success away from them.

I sometimes think if you're not very good at turning up for stuff and structuring stuff, but you are part of a team, then whether you have ADHD or not, you turn up because you don't want to let the team down. There's accountability, like with personal training. My partner says, 'How come when your trainer tells you to do stuff, you do it, and when I tell you the same thing, you don't?' and I say, 'Because I'm paying him: it doesn't make sense to pay him to tell me, and then ignore him.' The structure seems to be important. If you can get it from an app or create a plan and stick to it, great; otherwise, having another person to put that structure on you can help.

There's been quite a lot of research on exercise and ADHD, but it's been poorly carried out for the good reason that it's very difficult. We screened a thousand people for a final sample size of 160. I'd say half of the ones we screened were invited, but one of the downsides with ADHD is the logistics of getting to the lab. We've switched to a home experiment for our next study, and you still get three or four missed calls. One of my problems is that you can have many people with ADHD who all present completely differently yet have the same medication, the same form of exercise, and do the same things. There are excellent reasons to classify ADHD as we do currently, both for research and for clinical purposes. Like all conditions, you could split them up a million different ways if you wanted to, but how helpful is that, especially from a financial perspective, in managing treatments?

I started to think if you're hyperactive and impulsive, maybe cycling is better. And if you're inattentive, maybe yoga is better, but we don't know because nobody's looked, and people change. It's well known that hyperactive-impulsive symptoms tend to quieten as you get older, so can you have a quick symptom check to go, 'I'm having a week where I'm going to do some yoga, as opposed to a run'? We're a long way from that, and we haven't yet been able to pick it apart, but I'm pretty interested to see if we can get a dynamic symptom profile and see what kind of exercise helps.

The other worry with exercise is around dependence. You always see them on daytime TV, the heroin addict or alcoholic who runs a marathon, and their life changes. As somebody who runs marathons, I get it. But also, I get the fact that I follow a training plan and if I'm injured, I still follow that training plan, and that's really stupid. I'm getting slightly more sensible, but it's taken me eight marathons to get to the start line uninjured. If you are, in effect, prescribing exercise to a clinical population who are known to be more likely to encounter addictions, are you risking them hurting themselves or taking exercise to an unhealthy extreme?

That was partly why we started to look at exercise addiction and dependence, which is a controversial idea and very informally recognised. We did find that people with ADHD fixate more and are more likely to get a withdrawal from exercise, but they are not overall more likely to get exercise addiction in its entirety. Another study that hasn't been published yet finds that same thing again with a different population, which is quite reassuring, but also doesn't find they are more at risk of overuse injuries, which you would expect if you exercise when you're injured, or you're fixating more. In doing that, we found in the literature that people with ADHD struggle to quit smoking compared to those without. The withdrawal from nicotine is much harder for them, but not from cannabis, so it isn't an 'any drug' thing. I'm not sure what makes nicotine and exercise different from cannabis in this regard, but we'll see that as less of a problem because fewer people smoke these days.

Those withdrawal symptoms are there for everybody. You hear it a lot with the runner's high: a few weeks ago, I was tapering off before a marathon, and my partner said he could very much tell because I was grumpy. When you have that alongside ADHD, and you add in the other social and relationship challenges that often come alongside, I think it's worse.

One of the other motives for the research was this complete lack of parity between physical and mental health. My dad has various conditions of the kind that you get when you're older, and one is type 2 diabetes. He has a subsidised gym membership, which is great, and I'm all for that. But why don't you get a subsidised gym membership if you've got ADHD? Well, presumably, you don't get one because there isn't yet evidence that exercise is good for ADHD like there is for diabetes, so I get it, but it's more a lack of evidence rather than a lack of a case. For example, exercise is in the NICE guidelines for treating depression, but you don't get a subsidised gym membership if you're depressed. The literature shows that people with ADHD tend to have lower occupational functioning than those who don't, which means less disposable income, and yet they may stand to benefit much more from a gym membership. It's all very well saying, 'Go for a walk or go for a run,' but there could be plenty of reasons why that's not possible or not safe. The more evidence base there is, the more likely you'll be able to say, 'Okay, I can give you a prescription for methylphenidate, and I can also give you a subsidised gym membership for six months, see how you get on with it.' At its best, the NHS is brilliant, and we're very lucky to have it, but unfortunately, for various reasons, it isn't at its best. When a system is under strain, there has to come a point of asking individuals to take greater responsibility, but you can't ask them to do that if you haven't told them what may or may not help them. You're just sending out people with no idea of what would help them and saying, 'Have a go,' and that could make it worse. The more evidence we can get, the better.

CHAPTER SIX

Friends, families and relationships

When I was twenty-one, a friend said she couldn't be friends any more because it was too much work. After the call ended, I burst into tears and primal screamed in the sitting room. I have no idea where she got that idea from!

I find something profoundly awe-inspiring in people who have had the same friends for years. I have almost no friends from before university, and few from then, although two have also been diagnosed with ADHD. At thirteen, I was gently dumped by a school friend, and I still use her family's landline number for passwords because it's one of the few six-digit numbers I can remember. My brother has had the same friendship group since his teens; they are godparents to each other's kids. I wonder whether that is because they are all solid people who firmly knew who they were.

I was a shapeshifter, although I never meant to be. Even my accent changed depending on who I was with, my mannerisms often reflecting who I was speaking to so the group didn't feel uncomfortable. At university, I had friends for crosswords, music, musicals, choir, journalism and theatre, friends for chai, baguettes and hummus, friends for college, and friends for where I lived. Rarely did I have friends where I could bring all those things together. I joked that I was a Swiss Army knife, bringing out whichever trait, ability, or common interest I thought best fitted the situation. At one point, while I was on probation for missing all my morning classes – the result of my inability to drift off before 4 a.m. – I held twelve positions in my college. I was even playing in sports teams badly. I was high on sociability. I did everything I could to fill my time because it distracted me from the vertiginous horror that my mind inflicted when I was alone. It must have been like being friends with a panic-stricken PlayStation avatar.

I don't think I was a tomboy; I just found girls overly complicated. I was overly complicated, too, but there were so many layers that I either didn't like or couldn't understand. For a long time, I was more comfortable with boys in a deeply platonic way. I couldn't fit in with many girls, and boys didn't seem to mind. They just took me as I was. I must apologise for this next bit, which sounds like a parody of a gap year. When I was on holiday with a bunch of guy friends, I had a breakthrough about being a woman. We had all taken mushrooms – mine at a lower dose because I had the nineties horror of drugs instilled in me, along with quicksand and sparklers – and while the boys were in hysterics outside, leaping around, I was curled up inside the wooden summerhouse watching figures appear until the walls were filled with a chorus of womanhood. One was hanging out laundry. One was being taken from behind by an unseen lover.

Each had an unmistakable spark of self. It was suddenly so clear to me that every woman is a part of the universe in their special way. It wasn't what you looked like, what you did, what was happening. You just *were* as clearly and purely as the stars. Then I went on to have the standard 'Oh my God, we're all going to AGE, and wealth is so TRANSIENT' realisations and went to sleep. Still, that gorgeous moment of accepting that, whatever society told me, *I was a woman* has always stayed with me as something extraordinary. Understanding this led to me developing friendships with women, which was massively helped by finding enchanting and intense weirdos who also liked to swerve small talk. And if I wasn't around those people, there was always booze and food to help things along.

Unfortunately, some people are arseholes who identify somebody whose brain works differently and gently lean on them, perhaps not really knowing why, and then lean on them slightly more. As Tina Fey says in her poem 'The Mother's Prayer for Her Daughter', 'May she be beautiful but not damaged, for it's the damage that draws the creepy soccer coach's eye, not the beauty.' I had a few boyfriends like that, primarily because I was so surprised that anyone wanted to date me that I'd say an immediate yes and then spend the relationship codependently keeping it going, usually long past its natural sell-by date. Wanting people to be okay can be lovely. It becomes people-pleasing and flat-out madness if we do it in a dysregulated way. I first met my husband thirteen years before we started dating. He is a good, kind, joyful, clever and thoughtful man, entirely himself and at ease in the world. I am grateful every day that we didn't start going out until I was thirty.

Four years after I stopped drinking, I can still get quite anxious before going somewhere, even to lunch, through anticipating what might happen without alcohol as a prop. This is especially the case with large groups. Often, it's wonderful, and I have a lovely time – I was the chaos, not everyone else. It's like building muscle. I bank up more of these experiences and remember that I don't need to armour myself. I'm not a hermit crab any more. Just 100 per cent crab.

NAOMI, 26: The idea of ADHD wasn't even on my parents' radar. When I told them, my dad had a smelly attitude towards it, but that's fine. He's not my vibe, anyway. My cousins definitely have ADHD, and it's also clear that their parents and my parents do. They're not diagnosed, but I can tell that it's genetic. My youngest cousin would fall asleep anywhere out of boredom. When he was excited, he would not stop. My aunt was offended when the teachers tried to say he had ADHD, and she took him out of school. But that's because there's a fear of being othered and discarded instead of your needs being catered to. It's a difficult relationship because you want your children to have the best that they can, but if they're already being labelled for how they look, and then on top of that, add ADHD, so probably behavioural issues, it's very hard to come out of labelling in general.

CLARE, 42: Two friends have been diagnosed with autism and ADHD. We met at a hard house club at 5 a.m. or something ridiculous when we were twenty. We all got our diagnoses in the last two years. I keep reading about neurodiverse people tending to find each other and stick together, which has been true for me. I remember a friend once saying, 'I've never known anyone who can go from being on top of the world to jumping off the cliff in ten seconds like you.' It makes sense now because of emotional dysregulation, but at the time, it was, 'Clare is highly strung; Clare is high-maintenance.' It's comforting to know that it's not my fault, and it wasn't in the past. You can also use that to help other people when you start seeing it in them. I can see it in my mum and in my sister. My son's got his diagnosis; he's eight. I'm glad he's found out now because it means he is learning how to handle it. He won't miss all the opportunities I did.

ANDY, 52: When you don't meet other people's expectations, especially socially, they get hostile. Otherwise really lovely people would get sneery, and I'd think, 'What have I done?' If I overreacted or took things too personally, that emotional dysregulation would wind people up. I just seemed to irritate people, especially when stressed and angry. When I got diagnosed, I was like, 'Ah, that's what it was'. There's that famous quote that everybody's fighting their own battles that we know nothing about. I'm still pretty judgy with people; I try not to be, but it's a bad habit. I don't know what's going on in their life or their head, so I should give people the benefit of the doubt. Plenty of people out there are jerks, and they deserve our scorn, so let's reserve it for them.

ANNABELLE, 51: The difficult part was saying to my family, 'Look, this is why I was like that,' and they were a bit, 'Okay, yeah, whatever.' Now, I'm accepting that not everybody will understand what we go through on a day-to-day basis, and I'm okay with that. I wanted everyone to understand that I didn't mean to fuck my whole life up. Getting divorced and losing my children – even though we have the most incredible relationship now – there was a reason for this. In treatment, people had suffered abuse, so you could always correlate what had led them to blow up their lives. But I was just clueless. To finally know what it is and, more importantly than anything, to know other women who have ADHD and addiction issues is all I need to make me laugh, to make me cry. Just having someone that understands without thinking, 'God, you're such a freaking weirdo.'

BEN, 40: My friendship group has shrunk, but it's become more meaningful. Conversations and relationships are much more personal. I had a lot of superficiality around me and people who didn't have my interests at heart. I'm not expecting everyone to run around me, but I think there were many people I hadn't realised were using me and the friendship without being genuinely interested. Those people have slowly fallen away. I've reconnected with people that I haven't spoken to for a while. Equally, I may not see someone for months on end, and then as soon as I see them, it's like no time has passed, so those kinds of relationships have evolved. My relationship with my family has been challenging. I need to be more patient with them and see that their intentions aren't always negative. I need to be a bit kinder on what they've got going on in their lives.

INDER, 59: My wife told me to get out of bed and stop thinking. I can't help it. I wish I had normal thoughts; I wish people were normal to me, that I could just be happy. I have always been odd; I've noticed that. We had an arranged marriage when I was twenty-two, and she was eighteen. She's a wonderful person; luckily, I've ended up with someone good. I chose to study at Sheffield because that was where she was studying. I'm shocked that she's still with me. I told her that this weekend because it's coming up to this diagnosis appointment. She's been nasty occasionally, but who isn't? She's coming to terms with mental illness. There's a massive denial, being Indian: you deny that there's anything wrong in your family. My wife's brother was sectioned because he has schizophrenia; she had to help sort things out, yet this deniability remains.

I never knew I was brown growing up. No one ever told me. Then I suddenly found out. My rugby club was amazing; if anyone did anything, they'd be onto them. It was a great thing being looked after and having that love. When you've never had anything, you think everyone's nasty. They came to watch me playing at school and asked me to join them. Because we were a blue-collar club, everything was written off as drink talk; don't worry about it, we're all mates. I said inappropriate things, but they put it down to drink talk. In 1986, there were hardly any Indians playing, not many black players, and the ones playing were racially abused with bananas; it was really bad in those days. There was nothing other than pure white from the 'right side': you've got to be a public schoolboy or go to our old school to play for our club, old boy. My team had a West Indian of mixed heritage, a black guy, a Pakistani, me, and a good ol' boy from the Deep South. In 1986! Unheard of. I look at the photograph today, and that's how I survived. Rugby saved me. First, it got me back into education, then saved me when I was on a downer, and got me into work. It's been a second family.

FIONA, 53: I've had some toxic relationships because all I was doing was facilitating them. An old friend from school was almost angry when I got my breast cancer diagnosis. I love her to bits, but she's absolutely mad. Other friends said, 'She just won't acknowledge that you're ill.' And, of course, I'd always done everything for her. I'd always rushed to her side whenever anything happened. My mum mentioned it today. She said, 'You've got to remember she never came to see you once. She might have sent you treats and texts, but she drove past the house.' I backed off a bit, and of course, she was livid. I'm fifty-three, and I've only just worked it out. The best thing that ever happened to me was getting the cancer because it allowed me to filter out a whole load of crap. It dawned on me that I could only cope with so much because I had spread myself so thin before that, and I had to recover. In doing so, I've come out the other end, and there are many people I care for deeply who I've not reconnected with because I'm trying to help me. I'm a lot better in the last couple of years. It's been quite harsh to realise that time runs out, you know, for everybody. It's not that I'm going to fall off my perch tomorrow, but I've realised that I've neglected myself in trying to make things okay for everybody. I always did it from a positive place because I always wanted people to feel happy. And I now realise that there were certain individuals who – subconsciously, I think – could have exploited me.

SEAN, 38: One of my friends, who was later diagnosed, was my best friend in high school. We've known each other for coming up to twenty-eight years. We knew we were similar, but it didn't occur to us at eleven or twelve that we both had a condition that needed dealing with. We just knew we got on and would develop obsessions, flip from different things constantly, and play loads of video games together. In hindsight, it makes perfect sense that we both have ADHD.

CLEMENTINE, 36: I think the tedious term 'opposites attract' is spot on. My husband and I are so different. He was a professional musician, which is as similar as we get, which is lucky because God, if I had married another one of me, the mind boggles. We pull each other back on course in entirely different ways. He's the guy who would rather spend an hour in a supermarket looking for the correct kind of soy sauce than, God forbid, ask someone. I'm constantly embarrassing him because a) it takes so little and b) I am quite an embarrassing wife. But if I'm with him in the supermarket and we can't find the soy sauce, I will just go and ask. He recognises that some of my traits help him. He wouldn't ask for help in the supermarket; it would kill him. He recognises that in my approach to parenting, our girls are my little lion cubs, and they will grow up so proud of who they are. ADHD doesn't define who they are;

it is simply one of many, many components that makes up who they are. They have their own personalities, their own strengths and weaknesses and they also happen to have ADHD. Andrew and I try to use our strengths to offer the girls a balanced upbringing; I teach them to be passionate, confident and tenacious and Andrew shows them how to be calm, rational and considerate.

EMILY, 48: Since my ADHD diagnosis, I take way less shit. I went on a date nine months ago, and something was off from the beginning. I just stopped and went, 'You know what? We're done.' It must have been twenty-six minutes in. I could spend another two hours with this person I don't like, who's obnoxious and undermining everything I believe, because I would like to be perceived as being nice. Or I can accept that this isn't a rejection of me, just he's a dick, and you can move on. And my friends were gobsmacked. They were like, 'You've literally been in relationships with people because you didn't know how to get out of it!' I don't think I was medicated yet then, but I was already at a point of thinking that, as much as I want the dopamine hit of someone thinking that I'm a nice person, I'm worth more than that. I'm willing to take that hit away because this isn't the right thing for me. And I think that is totally a diagnosis thing to now understand why my brain would want to listen to you drone on for another hour, but, ultimately, that's because that's how my brain works, not because that's what I want.

HANNAH, 50: When my son was diagnosed in Year Five, I assumed it came from my ex-husband because he definitely has ADHD, although undiagnosed. I was seeing a therapist when we lived abroad about six years ago, and she said she thought I had ADHD, something I laughed off: 'I don't have ADHD. I'm organised!' I listened to Emma Mahony talking about ADHD on *Woman's Hour* and read more about it, and then my son said, 'You know, Mummy, I really think you do have ADHD.' I'm basically seeing myself through him, I began to realise, too. He doesn't like group situations, so we're both similar there. It's why I moved into counselling because it's one on one. When I'm in a group, I find groups deeply uncomfortable. I'm not very good at making small talk and like deep connections, but you can say things and afterwards think, 'God, did I say too much? Was I too revealing?' We both find some social cues difficult, such as what you're meant to do or say. I'd find those social niceties difficult. Small talk feels false. It's on the surface, and I'm not very good at putting on a mask. I'm not a game player. I'm not very good with people who are pretending to be nice and to have a chat. It just doesn't sit well with me. Now, I can see the lineage in my family and understand it a lot more. I understand why my mum was the way she was.

JAMES, 47: I've always been socially awkward, and most of that comes from ADHD. The analogy I use with people is, if you're hanging from a window ledge by your fingertips, you obviously don't want to fall, but eventually, your fingertips are going to give out. That is me in any conversation. It doesn't matter how much I want to listen or engage. At some point, my brain will just let go, and I'm going to fall, and there is nothing I can do about it. It makes conversing with people who aren't interesting very difficult. And because I find very few people interesting, which could be a personality flaw, it makes social interaction difficult. I have to be incredibly particular about who I hang out with, or I will come across as incredibly rude. I'm not listening; I walk away. I pull out my phone or something like that because I need something to get my brain going again.

I remember being out with my ex-wife and her friends when we were first dating. We'd gone to Leeds Castle and were sitting in a field. I'd been chatting to them for a while, and I turned to her and said, 'I need to go to sleep,' then lay down and dozed off. I had been talking to people who hadn't interested me for so many hours that I was exhausted. When I woke up, I was fine and could do it for a bit longer. I find that a real struggle, and I'm fascinated by how differently people with different types of ADHD experience those things. How much of it has to do with ADHD, and how much of it has to do with whether a person is extrovert, ambivert or introvert because all of this comes back to dopamine, right? I still don't know quite the best way to deal with that. I see friends more often in groups than one on one. Because with three people, the pressure is not on you to keep the conversation going. You can bow out of it if you need to. If your brain gets a bit frazzled, or if the fatigue starts to set in, you can kind of step back, do something else, and they can carry on, so it doesn't grind everything to a halt.

MICHELLE, 41: I tend to talk too much. It happens less at work, probably because I mask significantly, worried that I'll get something wrong or say something daft, but the people closest to me can't get a word in edgewise. Some friends don't mind that – 'I love listening to you. It's fine. Carry on.' With others, I need to stop and pull myself back from that hyperverbal communication.

Sometimes, I forget people exist. I look at a message and think, 'I will get back to it later, but I don't have the wherewithal to do it right now.' I still forget to message people back. I can go three months without talking to my parents. I only talk to them now because I have a routine that says every Saturday, I get in my car at quarter to eleven, and I call them on the way to my hoop class. My mum is undiagnosed ADHD, and she can talk at me something chronic, so I know I have a twenty-five-minute time slot where we can chat about everything and nothing.

NATALIE, 33: My main challenges are with emotional reg-ulation and RSD. The other day, I attended a friend's book launch alone, and on the train home, I suddenly felt really depressed and physically exhausted. I later realised I felt rejected as she barely spoke to me all night, which wasn't her fault; she was doing her job and having to sign books and meet people! I understand that now, but in the moment, I felt so alone, worthless and rejected. Maintaining a long-term relationship is also bloody hard, although I'm fortunate to have a supportive, kind, patient and tolerant partner.

DR TONY LLOYD: It was so obvious that I had ADHD, and my mother too. I remember being sent to the shop for cabbage and coming back with a mop head. My mother battered me with it. We were a very 'nice' family. Dad was an officer in the Navy. My mother had horrendous postnatal depression symptomatic of ADHD, and migraines, as did I, and she just did not have the capacity to be a parent to four children when Dad worked away at sea. I was an academically gifted kid who, of course, was lazy and didn't try hard enough. Nice bright kids were never considered 'those kinds of kids'. Who we are is the sum of so many things. ADHD is a facet, but it's not the total. It's remarkable how many kids thrive despite the battering that their self-esteem takes at school and at home when parents don't understand that the reason their child isn't doing as they're told is not because they're defiant but because they've not heard, forgotten it or haven't processed it.

THE PROFESSIONAL VIEW

SARAH CANNON-GIBBS is a psychologist in the NHS and private sector. She specialises in working with individuals and couples and was recently diagnosed with ADHD.

RSD is extreme. It's almost like an emotional sensitivity triggered by the perception that a person has been rejected or criticised. That might not even be their intention for the person on the other end, but it's just so painful for someone else. I notice it especially when working with couples with suspected ADHD or a diagnosis. It's almost like you're at cross purposes; each is misunderstood. The model I do with my couples looks at cycles and patterns. It's almost a dance. With ADHD, it's about co-regulation. Emotions love emotions. Carry on, and you're in fight-flight. The first part of our work is to de-escalate and learn to co-regulate as a couple. You have individual responsibility, and then you have responsibility within the couple. Self-soothing skills are important. DBT [dialectical behaviour therapy][12] teaches emotional regulation, distress tolerance and interpersonal skills, which help you say, 'Okay, I need to soothe myself before I can ask for what I need.'

---

12 'Dialectical behaviour therapy (DBT) is a type of talking therapy. It's based on cognitive behavioural therapy (CBT), but it's specially adapted for people who feel emotions very intensely.' https://www.mind.org.uk/information-support/drugs-and-treatments/talking-therapy-and-counselling/dialectical-behaviour-therapy-dbt/

Boundaries are important for looking after yourself and other people. With ADHD, we can struggle to enforce them because we don't even know what they are. We've never been taught. It isn't as simple as saying no because there will always be a consequence. That's another Instagram thing: 'Put in a boundary.' There's an impact, right? 'I'm too tired. I'm not coming to your birthday party.' Absolutely, look after yourself, but there may also be an impact on your relationship. Think about what you value and prioritise. Sometimes, we might have to overstep a boundary because we value something. Boundaries are movable. They are not a stagnant thing.

Looking at the nuance is important. It could be a family member telling you what to do in your parenting. It can be hard to say no because there's often a fear of the response. That's why attachment stuff is interesting to look at. It might be easier to say yes or no in one relationship than in another, and you've got to ask yourself: what is going on there that makes it hard to say no? It comes down to safety and security. If I feel secure enough to put in a boundary, I can do it, but if I don't have that safety, I can't. It's all very well saying, 'Say no, be strong, do it!' It might be unsafe, too, especially if we think about violent relationships.

You can have all the skills in the world, but if the person is unable to hear, help or respond, then it's fruitless. It's like going to a hardware store to get milk.

This is why things are relational. We can have a toolbox and go to the person, but you're back to square one if they have no insight, awareness or boundaries and may be abusive. That's why, when thinking about how it comes up in relationships, think about the cycle. Often, people don't know how to set a boundary because they don't know how to articulate it, so they make it about the other person. Then it's about being able to say instead, 'I'm feeling really uncomfortable, and I'm no longer going to engage in this conversation.'

Dr Russ Harris's work around ACT [acceptance and commitment therapy][13] looks at values and priorities in a lovely way. He uses a tool called The Wheel of Life, which looks at the variables that impact how hard we say yes and no. So much of that is linked to self-esteem, sense of self and sometimes indecisiveness, not knowing whether you should leave or go. The reality, too, sometimes: if you're in a relationship with financial commitments or children, what's the impact going to be?

---

13 'Acceptance and commitment therapy (ACT, which is pronounced as the word 'act') is aimed at helping you to take active steps towards building a rich, full and meaningful life, and at the same time, helping you to develop psychological skills to be able to deal with painful thoughts and feelings, in better ways so that they have much less impact and influence on your life.' https://www.likemind.nhs.uk/files/resources/Acceptance-and-commitment-therapy.pdf

PROFESSOR SUSAN YOUNG: Youngsters with ADHD can become sexualised earlier through using sex as a currency to gain social networks and friends. They often don't have good networks to go to for advice and have such poor coping strategies that they're at a loss as to what to do, how to handle things, and who to tell. Risk-taking behaviours and impulsivity can develop into sexually transmitted infections and early pregnancy. They can become young mothers, often single-parent mothers, and the cycle can build into their becoming the young mothers of ADHD children. With autism, there is often a misunderstanding of social cues, so they can be at additional risk of being abused.

Cheatsheet: How to be a good friend

Be flexible with boundaries. You don't have to be a people pleaser, but considering others is the bare minimum of being a person.

Types of therapy to look into:
- ACT (acceptance and commitment therapy)
- DBT (dialectical behaviour therapy)

Set annual birthday calendar reminders. A week before and two days before. This gives you the time to buy and send a present, or to forget, then still have time to send a card (or buy online), or to forget again but at least send a message on the day and panic order flowers.

A helpful tip my mum gave me is to add the year of birth to the reminder – especially helpful with godchildren and niblings when you never have any idea how old they are.

Random messages. If setting a regular reminder to contact a relative or friend feels overly strict, send random postcards, letters and texts when it occurs to you – it's very easy for months to go by without you realising it. My friend Will sends messages checking in, which is something I am always delighted by and which would never have occurred to me to do.

Keep things ticking over. If you are online, engage with your friends' updates and celebrations. Yes, it's basic, but it's good digital manners.

Find an ADHD community. Having people who 'get it' is incredibly helpful for navigating life, whether they live in your phone (Instagram, podcasts, WhatsApp and online ADHD groups) or face to face (therapists, coaches and friends).

On a practical level, it really helps to communicate to friends in advance that you have issues with certain things. You can always go back to, 'I know it was your birthday, and I didn't get you a present, but I've been thinking about it for weeks, and this is the specific thing I wanted to get you, I just couldn't get myself to do it in time,' so that they don't get hurt.

Be okay with losing friends who don't understand. Obviously, there's a need for patience, but I also think it's important to protect yourself from ideas that don't reflect who you really are.

– NAOMI, 26

CHAPTER SEVEN

Work

I've concluded that the best feeling is to be in the middle of your life, not thinking about the past or worrying about the future, only thinking about now. This is flow. It can be hyperfocus. It can be mindfulness, which is also why that is always suggested to people with ADHD. When you get it at the right time, it's glorious. When you don't, it's a nightmare. If countries could harness hyperfocus, stagnant productivity levels would no longer be an issue. More often, it has no control: Dr Hallowell describes ADHD as a Ferrari engine with bicycle brakes. This also explains my career. My CV is a series of ink blots hastily rewritten to suggest a considered path rather than a lurch from interest to interest or redundancy to redundancy. When I graduated, my parents sent me on an insight into management course, thus clarifying my suspicion that I had no desire to manage anyone. I felt like a pigeon among penguins. I couldn't function in that world. I needed to find somewhere interesting;

otherwise, I would sink and never get out. I had no idea how you got a job somewhere you liked, so I entered competitions. I longed for a mentor. If moving to the sewers and taking up with a sentient rat would have helped me navigate work and life, I might have seriously considered it.

My dad worked at the same firm throughout his career, the company changing its name around him as he moved up the ranks. I have never had a promotion and have been made redundant four times in my first eleven years. In journalism, 'going freelance' is often a euphemism for losing your job and needing some work to tide you over while you look for another. When I first 'went freelance' at twenty-four, I was fined a hundred pounds for not declaring this to HMRC, a considerable sum to me whose previous salaries wavered between thirteen and sixteen thousand. It simply hadn't occurred to me to look it up. Subsequent tax returns were done in tears, usually at the last minute, on the back of an A4 piece of paper, with minimal receipts to claim because I had mislaid the envelope into which I'd been stuffing them.

I steadily filled gaps and accrued skills at work to make myself indispensable. It wasn't enough to be an online journalist; I would also write reviews and the advice column. I learned how to write scripts, and to film and edit the tapes. I wrote news stories and live blogs and found stories through Twitter. I covered shifts on various desks, presented videos, and shyly pitched stories to the supplements. Whatever was needed, I learned how to do it – perfect freelancer training, although I didn't realise that then. Everyone had a clearly defined role, beat and interest. I told myself I did loads of stuff, so I wasn't serious. Perhaps it was that constant feeling of not being quite right, but I was drawn to security because I assumed that is what it takes to be all right in the world. I moved from permanent job to permanent job, but each time, I either wanted more from it or was made redundant. I made sensible choices, and I made ones that weren't. My most ADHD decision was resigning from a job on a whim because I'd been offered a freelance column to write about the long-running BBC radio soap *The Archers*, one of my favourite obsessions. The column was online-only, terribly paid, and the commissioning editor left a few weeks after I started, after which my column died, too. I'd felt the urge to take it partly because I always wanted to write a column about *The Archers* but also because this offer came a couple of months after the failed IVF. I was feeling dizzily aware of no longer needing a job that offered maternity leave, even though I needed a job that paid more than the column. Such are the flights of logic I encountered.

Being neurodivergent at work feels like that bit in *The Wrong Trousers* where Gromit is frantically laying out the track in front of him as the train roars along. What has been a constant firefight for the individual is now a learning moment for businesses. Many people I've spoken to have said that their biggest challenge is that, now they can have support, they just don't know what to ask for or how to ask for it. What is a 'reasonable accommodation'? Gen Z have different workplace expectations from Boomers, Gen X and Millennials, who usually just suck it up without complaint before burning out. I left the workplace altogether, preferring to zip in and out for short periods without getting drawn into office politics. Freelancing works because I can have a lie-down without worrying about presenteeism if I need to rest. Ironically, it also means I don't take enough breaks due to ongoing worry about work or getting things done. My last staff job had a quiet room labelled, 'This is not for sleeping.' By the afternoon, I would often be so exhausted that I needed to be somewhere quiet, but I'd sit worrying that somebody might come in. Lighting was also an issue. I went to sleep in starkly lit rooms, whether in university lectures or office meetings.

At least now there are tools like Calendly for booking meetings and automatically syncing them with my Zoom account and diary, and Otter, which records and auto-transcribes conversations, saving writers from the twin hells of transcription and listening back to themselves. Word-based admin can be challenging for everyone. I am a qualified sub-editor skilled at working with others' copy. Still, my brain can skip blindingly obvious errors in my own, which can feel like I'm gaslighting myself and others about my abilities. The Grammarly plug-in which Cat Harris highlights later in the chapter has been a godsend. 'It's just always there' is one of the most significant organisational inventions of the twenty-first century. Before online storage, I could forget something almost as soon as I saved it. I couldn't afford software subscriptions, so I rarely used spreadsheets and found the language used to control them completely unintuitive. The introduction of Google Sheets and Docs meant that I could make a basic spreadsheet to track my freelance jobs, payments and invoicing and save it to my bookmark bar so that I never lost it. As banking improved, I moved my invoicing to a mobile business account, which meant that, in a few clicks, I could send these details to the accountant that I could finally pay for (and, crucially, write off against tax). I set calendar reminders for deadlines a week and two days beforehand, and I wish you could set more. I need five-minutely reminders for meetings because if I don't go into the Waiting Zone, I will forget – I missed an interview for my own book because I forgot after the first alarm. Still, the Waiting Zone is a profoundly unhelpful compensation. For subsequent interviews, I would stare at my computer for half an hour to ensure I wouldn't miss them. If I have a meeting, there is a good chance that I will achieve absolutely nothing beforehand because all I can think about is not missing it. Being aware of both aspects means that I try to do the thing at the first reminder because if I don't, I have mentally downgraded its importance, and it's unlikely to get done. When my watch nudges me to take my afternoon meds, I have to do it immediately because if I think, 'I'll do that in a minute,' two hours will pass.

NAOMI, 26: There's a paradox of wanting to get something done but not being able to get yourself to do it because your brain is disabled and needs specific accommodations. I don't know what these accommodations are, especially as someone who's just started my career. I won't know until I fail, essentially, and that can really knock your confidence. People often assume I will take ownership of organising projects and tasks. I've had to train my brain to do that. When something is stimulating, I do it well; when it's not, it's hard to get myself to do it. Easy mistakes make me look careless, but I definitely care; I reread this three times. I missed that error because my brain skipped it.

It's hard when you are stuck; you don't know the solution, or you would have asked for it. You need someone almost to coach you out of those moments. If they had that skill, the problem would stop existing; it's that simple. Instead, my manager became super conscious of any time I didn't do something and treated me as if

I were lazy, and that was a narrative that carried on. I would overwork or work overtime because I didn't want to be seen in a certain way.

Training for managers working with neurodivergent people is really important. As long as people are part of your plate, you have to accommodate them. My managers have opposed that because they say, 'It's not my job. I'm not taking on anybody else's responsibilities.' There needs to be more clarity around it being a shared responsibility. If you don't take any, you're not being accommodating, and you're making somebody who's already disabled feel bad about their disability and making it harder for them to grow, which is irresponsible and mean. It should be mandatory that you have specific training and coaching if you have a neurodiverse person on your team. Even if you're not neurodiverse, you'd benefit from coaching: my cousins come to me about their struggles, and I sit with them and work out the problem, and then we get to a solution, as opposed to going, 'You just need to do XYZ,' which doesn't help. Access to Work gave me funding for an ADHD coach, which has been phenomenal. I use notion.com for mind-mapping because it's readily accessible. I start my working day with a list, which gives me peace of mind as I'm not relying on memory alone. I click on my calendar multiple times a day to tell me where I'm at and when because of time blindness. I don't use reminders because they do nothing for me; my brain just goes, 'Okay, notification!'

If I can't get myself to do something, I ask myself: is it because this is boring or overwhelming? If it's boring, I'll drink sparkling water, eat crunchy snacks, put on a song, and then stand up and dance while doing it to make it easier and more engaging and stimulating. I used to struggle with data input, and I've always played this one soothing song I like while I did it. Even now, if I'm in bed and can't get myself to get up and shower, I play that song. I could do something I didn't want to do and still enjoy the process because I like the song and trained myself. If the thing I'm avoiding is overwhelming, I figure out the two or three most important things, break them down into tasks, and work out how many minutes each step will take. It makes it feel less big because I realise this task I've been avoiding all day will probably not take more than an hour.

ANDY, 52: I never fitted into the nine-to-five office job grind. I'm nocturnal and would go to bed at 4 a.m., so the rush-hour commute was just hellish. Sitting in a shared workspace with people I didn't respect telling me what to do was like trying to change gears without pressing the clutch. One of the main reasons I went freelance was because I can't work like that. If somebody will pay me to make stuff up, that's better than sitting in front of a spreadsheet for some suit I don't like. If my brain doesn't find it engaging enough, it becomes incredibly difficult to do the work. If I can't do the work, I don't get paid because

I don't have a salary: in comics, we get paid by the page. Most of my work has been for hire, so it's not like I'm Robert Kirkman getting *Walking Dead* money. Everybody's waiting for me because the artists need the script to draw. If I'm not producing, then I can't pay the bills. There were times when I was living on my overdraft for years on end, and what with paying the mortgage and a family to feed, it was stressful. Had I known about ADHD, I could have made better choices.

The key was in an Edward Hallowell book, *Delivered from Distraction* [co-authored with John Ratey], where he described ADHD as an interest-based nervous system, so when you're trying to do something you're not interested in, it's like trying to roll a boulder up a hill. That has been revelatory for me. I've struggled to write scripts if I'm not engaged, even if it's high-profile and good for my career. If I'm not interested, I can't write, which is ridiculous because I've got deadlines, and I get well paid for it. At the time, it's quite scary. It happened to me ten years ago, and I struggled to figure out what was wrong. Why is this so difficult? Am I depressed? What's going on? The flip side was my university dissertation, where I sat down and wrote twelve thousand words the night before handing it in. I didn't start until 8 p.m., and I got my best mark ever because it was a subject I was interested in.

The nearest thing I've got to a toolkit is what I say yes or no to. The way I articulated it before I got diagnosed was that my head was always wrong, and my heart was always right. My head said if I wrote [redacted], that would be well paid, high-profile, and good for my career. But my heart and gut were like, 'Yeah, but you don't really give a shit about [redacted].' I've learned to trust my gut feeling because it knew what it was doing.

CLEMENTINE, 36: My mother is a musician, and my grandfather was a musician, so I was always going to be one too. My mum tried to get me to practise as a little girl, and she couldn't understand why I didn't want to because I love playing. I found it not terribly difficult, and I enjoyed the outcome. In hindsight, the thought of sitting in a room and practising alone was just the most diabolical brain-numbing thought. I went to a specialist music school from very young until I was eighteen, where it wasn't an option not to. There were members of staff specifically to check that you were in your practice room and you were practising. I'd kick up a fuss, but it wasn't a choice.

As soon as I was allowed to spread my wings, I didn't practise as much, which is so sad. It's purely down to a lack of knowledge about ADHD. What I needed was someone to sit down and spoon-feed me: 'Right, Clem, this week you need to practise that bar for intonation and that bar for the cadences.' You won't get that treatment at degree level because it's considered babyish, but that's how my brain works. I need things broken down. I happily would have hyperfocused on those points because I had that guidance.

I found marketing interesting as a student and thought, 'I'll start a business.' I would go to the big bookshop on Tottenham Court Road and read every single book on business, obsessed in my happy world. Thankfully, the company is still going: I provide string trios and quartets for events and pick which ones I want to play as a freelance musician. I created this world where I was in control. I didn't have to answer to anyone, which I've always struggled with, and I was managing the chaos I didn't know was in there. Pre-diagnosis, it would trouble me that people would say I was doing too much. I'd always say I wasn't doing too much. I'm doing what they consider too much. It wasn't because I was a super genius; it's just how I worked. When COVID struck, no one wanted a string quartet, so I looked for anything I could do and found an advertisement for a school looking for an arts administrator, which is now my other hat. Then COVID passed, and I was happy there as I was invested in everything. I'm not someone who could do a job I wasn't passionate about. I guess that makes me sound a bit needy and tedious, but I genuinely couldn't. I'd just quit.

HANNAH, 50: I used to work in business travel. Really fucking boring. The thing I struggled with was getting up in the morning. I got sacked from so many jobs because of it. I never used to be able to go to sleep, so I'd be up till two o'clock in the morning, worrying about all the things I might have done and said, and then I'd have to get up at seven to go to work. Or, deciding on Sunday night that it was a good idea to go out and get pissed. Trying to live a normal life was crazy when I felt like such an un-capable adult. I really enjoy the job I'm doing now, which makes all the difference; I'm doing something that I want to do rather than something that just pays the bills. I'm quite good at mornings, too; I'm disciplined about bedtime, and I can get to sleep, which is amazing to me.

JAMES, 47: I compare my brain to an old Triumph motorcycle. When it's running, it'll fucking fly down the motorway, and you'll have the best time ever. But when you go out on a cold winter morning, it is a fifty-fifty chance that fucker will start or not. And that is how I feel whenever I sit down to write; I might be able to write, I might not, and I don't know until I try. If it's a day where I can't, nothing I do will change that. Nothing. I just have to say, 'You know what, that's not going to happen today, I'm going to go off and play a game'.

When I'm given a deadline, I start it well in advance because if I've got five days to write something, at least two of those days will be write-offs, so I have to build that into the time I have. I've just learned to do that because that's what it is. I wrote a video game review yesterday. The night before, I spent four hours trying to make it work: I couldn't even get a paragraph done. The next morning, I breezed through it in ten minutes because my brain was cooperating on that day. What are you gonna do? I find crises quite appealing. It sounds awful, but obviously as an ADHD person my constant quest is, 'give me all the dopamine'. I find crises give you dopamine so when something happens, I'm brilliant, and I come into my own – let's get this shit done. That, I like. Give me a dozen minor tasks and it will kill me. I've been in my job for over twenty years, so people give me a certain amount of slack, but I don't listen in meetings, ever, and that is just understood. If anyone wants me, they say my name and then ask the question. It's not personal; this is how my brain works but I've worked here long enough that I can do that. If you're starting a new job, that's a very difficult thing to do.

CLARE, 61: I lived on deadlines: the adrenalin and cortisol meant I could focus on tiny details and work fast and accurately. Without them, I could miss obvious errors or forget important meetings. I was good in crises because I instinctively knew what to do, took charge, and did it. It was never the wrong action as I was hyper-aware of my limitations and didn't put myself or anyone else in danger. I could work on a problem until it was fixed as I either loved the challenge or was very stubborn.

MICHELLE, 41: I can't have a conversation with someone well above me in the hierarchy without being prepared, just so that I don't sound like a muppet. I was once asked to present to my team and could see people drifting off because I was rambling. My director was in the back making cut signs. Now, I will spend around three days preparing for a twenty-minute meeting. I have perfected the art of writing in a conversational style, so if it's a Teams meeting or Zoom, I can look back and forth but just read directly. If I'm on stage, I will make sure I've got some impactful stuff to say and my iPad to hand to ensure I'm getting to the right points.

I know other people who will prepare but not go through the same anxiety. I spend inordinate amounts of time on it, otherwise I worry and ruminate afterwards. 'Did I say that right? Wrong? Oh God, are they going to give me the sack?' Then, when you go off on a tangent, you're so panicked by it that you don't get to your point, whereas if you took a step back – and you know hindsight, wonderful thing – maybe you'd get it back.

I'm very lucky to have a wonderful manager. When I was assessed for ADHD, she jumped on it and contacted HR to find out what support was available. They went through Access to Work, and I got coaching sessions. My workplace did a further assessment, which allowed me to have these incredibly pricey noise-cancelling earbuds which I'm terrified of losing. The noise level coming down immediately calms me if I'm feeling overwhelmed. They also gave me access to this software, RSI Guard, which is supposed to stop me from working so that I take breaks, but I am so confused by the process to get it that I haven't managed to sort it. It's an ADHDer's nightmare. I love a good process. This is my job. But if you give me something I don't understand, I procrastinate.

The office is interesting. It's beautiful, all mod cons, everything you'd want from a big company. The challenge is the lights. I don't even know how to describe them, they're just there. After a few hours, I start feeling overwhelmed because of the lights, the noise, the fact I will try and work through when my medication wears out or forget that I need to take it. I find myself booking myself into dark rooms just so I can have peace and quiet. The office is not meant for someone like me who cannot cut sensory information out. It's worse in winter because then the lights are really in your face, but in summer, I have this time-blind tendency to work through, then look up and realise I should have left an hour ago. So, although the office is lovely, spacious and very welcoming, it's not built with a neurodiverse person in mind. I expect many people have the same challenges; they just don't understand what they are because it's not spoken about as much: 'It's just me; I'll just go to another area.' If businesses could understand a bit more about the impact of light, noise, temperature, or any of those things, it might be easier to work. On the one hand, I love going to the office to see my colleagues. On the other hand, I dread it because I know the next day, I'll be exhausted from putting that smile on my face and masking. I will have internal meltdowns where I bite my lip, nod, agree and smile, but inside, I'll want to throw staplers at people and it's not pleasant.

SEAN, 38: I'm often in situations where someone will say, 'Sean knows about that' or 'Sean can do that'. No one expects you to be that multiskilled, especially in local government. You do one thing, and that's it. Hobbies or other skills are just not really discussed.

CLARE, 42: I work in recruitment, so I sit on LinkedIn all day, and last year, someone I follow posted about Access to Work. I started the process in December, and after about four months, I spoke to a lovely lady who recommended a specific coach she said was perfect for postmenopausal women. I've got twelve sessions once my paperwork comes through, and she also recommended mental health coaching for someone who's been diagnosed later in life because that'll help with the masking, the grief, with all that kind of acceptance. They've also recommended noise-cancelling headphones and software, and I'm looking forward to seeing how that will help because I work with people all over the world and I've woken someone up before by ringing them in the wrong time zone in Canada. They'll also coach my managers on how to help me, things like 'don't micromanage' because I'll explode. If I feel like that, I stop working, stop talking, don't do anything. I struggle with noise. I was at an end desk, so I'd have people coming up behind me, and there were a lot of loud people who liked the sound of their voices. One person would touch my desk every time he passed by, and it drove me mad. Now I've got a desk right in the corner. It's got two windows. It's perfect. No one can come up behind me; I can see where everyone is, and it's so much better. I'm quite lucky that one of our MD's sons has ADHD, so he's keen to learn what he can do to help me. The headphones will help because now I'm aware of it, the noise is more difficult. I've also got some really good Loop earplugs. I wore them to my friend's fortieth the other week. We can be loud when we get together, especially when the others start drinking, so I put them in before I went. You can still hear; they just take the edge off. I also have sleeping ones for if I go anywhere new. Otherwise, it's all about organisation. I have a book of lists, and I do a day plan every morning of what I need to do and who I need to call. We've got a database CRM system but I like it to be written down so I can physically tick it off with my pen. If it's on the list, it'll get done. If it isn't, it's got no chance.

BETHAN, 42: In my agency, a third of the time I build in for everyone is 'fannying around' time. It's important that we put together realistic proposals and budgets so that everybody can work at a not-ridiculous pace. I'm very open with my freelancers that if we've run out of time, that's it; and we've got to flag that to the clients.

I have a 'ways of working' document between me and the client, which tells them the days and hours I work, when I'm available for calls and how many meetings I'm happy to have every week. I have my Zoom time between three and six thirty. I could easily work until two in the morning, so I set an alarm to stop myself and have dinner. That's after a year where I sat on Zooms all day every day and had a breakdown at the end. I can't do that, and I don't want to. It's too much information to process, and you can't do any work.

I've been fighting to shake off the corporate conditioning that you've got to work really hard, nine till five. If you run your own business, you can build it so work doesn't have to be hard; work can just be work. I have been able to build it in a way where I can get the right people to support me. That's why we're also based on a freelance model, so I can stop killing myself over writing huge research documents when I know a journalist who can write twenty pages in a tenth of the time it would take me, and it'll still be better! I can pull the interesting bits out of it for a press release, but writing a whole thing, I would drag it out over a long weekend like the carcass of a hangover.

I have a virtual assistant who works ten to twenty hours a month on things like calendars. I don't work Monday mornings or Friday afternoons unless it's something fun. On Tuesdays, Wednesdays and Thursdays, I'll have meetings from ten until two with a break for lunch. I do my invoices with my VA on the last Friday of every month. I cannot break Finance Friday because I find it so boring and when I was doing it by myself, I ended up not doing it and not getting paid. I was paying everyone else, but I'd only have eighty pounds left. I've built in all these structures, and I tell my assistant: these are my boundaries;

I am crap at respecting them, so you have to respect them for me. She even builds stuff into my calendar like, 'Do to-do list for the next day' and 'Clock off'.

AL, 41: My dad says my job is like being in *Thunderbirds*. It works quite well with ADHD because a lot of it is crisis stuff: got to get eighteen people out the door with equipment and make sure they're safe. Some days are quite steady; yesterday was completely manic and my head was on fire. It's that mix that's kept me engaged. If someone comes to me on a Friday afternoon and says, 'I need to be in Kazakhstan for three weeks on Sunday,' I can turn that round in two hours, sewn up, done, dusted. I can do more work in thirty minutes if it's something that I'm engaged in than I can in three weeks if I'm not.

I fell into this job completely by accident. I didn't know what I wanted to do with my life. I was supposed to be a temp and now I've been here twelve years. My psychiatrist said she sees so many women that get to the stage of their careers where they're starting to do more managerial project work, and then they go, 'Oh, hang on a minute, I can't do this.' It just rang true. I liked the 'go go go' kind of stuff, but it wasn't doing my mental health any good. I had three and a half months off last year because I burnt myself out completely.

THE PROFESSIONAL VIEW

What can neuro-inclusivity at work look like?

CAT HARRIS is Head of Learning and Development (UK/Ireland) and Neurodiverse and Disability Lead at MediaBrands UK/Ireland.

Those entering the media industry now are more open about their requests and experiences, which we millennials and earlier generations are still a bit hazy about. People don't know whether they want to have a diagnosis. I read a piece by Dr Nancy Doyle of Genius Within in which she said, 'If people think they're neurodiverse, they probably are.' I thought that was quite powerful because I am left-handed and have self-diagnosed with dyscalculia. If I were to do an official assessment, I'm confident of that outcome, but that self-diagnosis helps me to think: 'That's okay, I'm the way I am, and these adaptations help.'

Schools are becoming better at supporting neuro-divergent people, but they can be thrown back into the Dark Ages when they enter employment. There should be accessibility questions when businesses open their doors to recruitment because they have a responsibility to their employees. Let's say you've got ten people with ADHD; their experiences will differ. We have amended our application process so that people can request reasonable interview adjustments through a named team member in HR. We use an app called Spark, so they can record a video in their own time introducing themselves and answering questions on screen. We're also considering whether we send questions to a candidate beforehand. If you are autistic, those surprises could impact your interview because you could come across as underprepared, whereas actually, you just can't answer on the spot.

We have a neurodivergent employee resource group, and many of our changes positively impact all staff. We are introducing quiet working spaces in all our offices with rules respecting the people there: perhaps they're overstimulated or want to concentrate on writing a report. We have core working hours, which is helpful for anyone wanting the flexibility of travelling in later to avoid rush hour. Every employee has free access to the Grammarly app, a little icon on your screen to help rephrase sentences and grammar. I always try to make my meetings start at five minutes past the hour. It's a simple technique because sometimes you can be in back-to-back meetings, and that's tiring for everybody, particularly those with ADHD who haven't got time to decompress and gather their thoughts before stepping into the next one. That's a cultural shift – people still turn up at four and go, 'Where is everyone?' – and that's because we're trying to learn the ropes. It's about accepting that not everybody can work at that speed or the brain can't always jump from project to project.

If I need a wee, and I'm in a meeting and I haven't got time, all I'm thinking about is how much I need a wee. I'm not present. Presenteeism is so hard over virtual meetings anyway; let's make sure people are as comfortable as possible.

We're about to launch manager training to cover common neurodivergences because you don't know what you don't know. It's about asking, 'What can we do to support you? What does a good working day look like? When are you most lit? Are you an a.m. person or a p.m. person?' Getting to know people is important, and some of the training I deliver is as basic as checking in with your team members and asking them how they are.

Cheatsheet: How to focus in the workplace

Email hygiene: Switch off pop-ups, sounds and notifications for anything other than your calendar. Set diary reminders to check your email regularly.

Create email filters for non-essentials like press releases, adverts and cc'd or bcc'd conversations so they bypass your inbox and go straight to a separate folder. It keeps your inbox clear, limits superfluous distractions, and you can deal with random clutter in one go.

Outsource as much admin and memory as possible. If an app or a calendar can do it, let it.

Apps and software:

- **Grammarly:** A free (and not annoying) cross-program plug-in that suggests spelling and grammar improvements and catches what speedy minds can miss. I started using it after speaking to Cat and am so besotted with it I've forked out for the paid version.

- **1Password:** Creates and stores all your logins so you can create and use secure passwords rather than the only ones you can remember.

- **Otter:** Transcribing software, which is excellent for recording and writing up calls and meetings, although so-so on recognising certain accents.

- **1Tap Receipts:** Take a photo or forward an email to this app and say goodbye to envelopes of receipts you inevitably lose.

Workplace suggestions:

- **Management training:** You don't know what you don't know, and neither do they.

- **Noise-cancelling headphones:** or noise-minimising products such as **Loops** help cut out some of the background noise that can be distracting.

Brown noise is comforting and helps me focus; I put a YouTube video on in the background. The Forest app and Pomodoro method help me get into a task and putting my phone in black-and-white mode helps minimise the 'shiny things' effect of technology.

– CAROLINE, 35

I ask for the accommodation or understanding I need rather than medicalising the reason: 'I find people constantly walking into my eyeline very distracting, so I'm more productive working from home' or 'I get tired when I'm in full "people" mode all day, so I need to make sure I don't have too many of those days in a row.'

– KATHLEEN, 29

Access to work

- In England, Scotland and Wales, you are eligible for government support through Access to Work if you are employed or self-employed – this is another confusingly named scheme, and it is not for people who are looking for work.

- You don't need a diagnosis. You do need to provide clear information about how ADHD affects your ability to work, and a general idea of what support would help you.

- Apply online [gov.uk/access-to-work] or over the phone [0800 121 7479]. You will need your employment details or self-employment details such as National Insurance and UTR numbers.

- After you submit your application, you will have a phone appointment to chat about what support would most help you, with suggestions from your Access to Work contact. If this is approved, you will receive a written pack a few months later with details of your grant. Mine took five months to come through.

- If you are employed, your employer will foot some of the bill so you will go through this process with them. If you're self-employed there are companies who help with the application process which can be helpful to look into – I rather wish I had, as chasing things up is a monumental time-suck especially when you are dealing with actual work.

- The process is very slow and keeping track of it all can be extremely challenging. This is where the ADHD sense of justice comes in useful. It is your right to have this support. Keep at it out of sheer cussedness. Let getting this support be your hyperfocus. You have paid for it in both official tax and ADHD tax. Yes, getting it is a pain in the arse but it will come eventually.

- **Tip:** Unless you have made specific arrangements with Access to Work due to hearing difficulties, it is better to communicate via phone than email. An ATW advisor told me the email account isn't checked very often, which explains quite a lot.

- **Tip:** If self-employed, **you do not need to front up ten grand yourself before getting your support.** Yes, you can pay for it yourself and then have it reimbursed, but Access to Work can also pay for sessions, software, etc., in advance. However, they will usually only pay for two sessions' worth in advance.

CHAPTER EIGHT

Organisation

My mother-in-law told me a lovely thing she'd heard from the late artist Philip Hicks: 'In routine lies freedom.' This may as well be tattooed on my hands. Being organised makes up for my brain being operated entirely by the baboons of chaos. I am an organised person, much like an air traffic controller is organised. If I use the set routines and systems, everything is fine. But if I deviate in any way, everything risks crashing down, and that's if it takes off at all. In some ways, I appear remarkably on top of things, but this is entirely due to systems, routines and reminders, without which I am an amorphous blob floating on the tide.

I used to believe that tidiness and organisation were character traits, like being vague, absent-minded, scatterbrained or careless, rather than skills I could learn with step-by-step instructions. It hasn't been a case of reaching a certain age and suddenly becoming capable, more of things being invented that have made it infinitely easier. The general idea of 'being organised' can be bewildering, whereas breaking it down into specifics makes it manageable and easier to understand – something that KC Davis does so well in her Struggle Care TikTok account and her book, *How to Keep House While Drowning*. Being overwhelmed by clutter often goes hand in hand with feeling out of control. Decluttering does not mean we're going to suddenly turn into rampant minimalists living alongside a single olive perched on a shelf. Many people find their brains ping off visual clutter; if things have a place, it lessens the pinging and the risk that you eventually stop noticing it's there. There is a lovely acronym for those mountains of mess that appear out of nowhere and then hang around – DOOM piles: Didn't Organise, Only Moved. I have one staring at me now, which started as a pile of things I want to get framed and now has any old crap on it waiting to be allocated a place to live.

As millions have done, I learned how to organise from Marie Kondo. Her system stuck because I loved her, and it made sense. It's a dream for minds that need order to combat chaos. In 2014, while my industry hit click targets by yelling that Kondo wanted everyone to get rid of everything they loved, I was lapping up her recommendations on clutter and clothing. Folding clothes vertically so you can see what you have – genius! Hanging what you can't fold – obviously! My cupboards and drawers are a tessellation of shoeboxes with my clothes, neatly visible and easily managed. I drew the line at unpacking my handbag each day, but her systems taught me how to appreciate what I had and show it off so that my mind always lands on something that gives it pleasure. She was also clear that you must do so in a way that makes sense for your life. I am that person who stores their books by colour and height – it feels calming to the eye; I know each by sight, and it breathes life and respect into even my oldest, crumbling paperbacks and so into me.

During the lockdowns, I boredom-bought stuff. When the time came for a clear-out, I remembered how much I loathe the process of online selling and posting, and with the charity shops closed, I used the garden wall as a freebie table. Baking equipment? Gone. Books? Gone. Half-used pots of fence paint? An automated cat feeder? The rubbish exercise bike I bought in March? Everything went. Now and then, organising and my desire to spend money overlap. I was thrilled to discover that my friend's brother was a carpenter and could make me a Little Free Library to go next to the freebie wall. Nick was duly hired and made the most beautiful house out of repurposed bits of wood he'd kept from jobs over the years, including trees he had felled and seasoned himself. The library makes me so happy; it gives another life and purpose to my books and more connection with my neighbours. I am hooked on the BBC TV show *Sort Your Life Out*, which features a lot of ADHD households, and hired a firm run by its organiser, Dilly Carter, for a day to sort out the attic, which doubles as an office and had become the house's portrait of Dorian Gray. Between that, the wall and the charity shops, everything is sorted for where to declutter things, and seeing what I have means I don't blindly shop online as much – more on that in the chapter on self-medicating.

When we find a eureka moment of understanding, it can be interesting to look back and observe how often we have built support around ourselves without knowing why. For years, I couldn't keep hold of my keys. I lost seven sets during my second year at university, one lot thrown away with shopping bags. My parents bought me an enormous wooden wedge keyring with THE BLOODY KEYS painted on in bold, which I managed to keep until it fell apart. My keys now go into a big dish in the kitchen as soon as I get home. My handbag goes on the side. The keys can't stay in the bag because otherwise they will float into a coat I don't wear again for eight months. Many of the things I now rely on came from my tech-enthusiast husband. He introduced me to Tile and AirTags, and my handbag and keys now have one each. My phone and watch have Find My Phone features linked to the bag and keys so I can play a sound to track them down. He also introduced me to the CityMapper and Waze apps, which are invaluable for navigating public transport and driving routes, and OurHome, which has a list of household tasks allocated to each of us, with points that gamify chores. He set up Alexa Echos and Dots throughout the house, which are great for timers, reminders and *The Archers*, and link up to smart plugs, light bulbs and the thermostat so there isn't that end-of-the-day faff of remembering which lights you've forgotten about. My glasses cases have their spot, but I've yet to find a solution for misplacing the glasses themselves. They are too thin to hold an AirTag and fall victim to my tendency to put them down, immediately forgetting where, plus now I can't see. While having my photo taken to announce this book, I removed my glasses, put them on a wall, and didn't realise I'd done so until I had travelled eighty miles out of the county. They were not there when I got back, and yes, I was medicated at the time. The current and very unsatisfactory solution is for me to call up to my husband and ask to borrow his eyes, like the Pale Man in *Pan's Labyrinth*, but more annoying. I'm looking into Orbit, a very small AirTag equivalent for glasses that syncs with the Apple Find function. I apologise to Android enthusiasts, but I've been wedded to Apple since my last Sony Ericsson Cyber-shot died. If it's any consolation, my browser is Chrome. I'm not a monster.

A godsend has been those developments in tech that automate and outsource. My phone instantly became an extra limb, so I've never lost it. I always use the calendar function – no more gorgeous paper diaries that trail into empty pages. Then Twitter let me bridge the gap between my incomprehension of networking and wanting to find people to work with. A couple of years ago, I bought a second-hand Apple watch to have my reminders burned into my wrist. It's essential now, partly because I'd always wanted an Apple watch and having the thing I wanted rather than its approximate gives me a stream of self-validation and pleasure, and partly because its haptic reminders give you a physical nudge instead of screeching out noises that flood you with adrenalin.

Until technology picked up, I was constantly panicking about where things were, what I needed to have done, when, and why I hadn't done it. Meals, grocery shopping and general life admin were dependent on the wind, so going out carousing made me feel less inadequate, if even more broke. My attitude to cooking was either toast or incredibly intricate meals for ten. I was amazed by people who brought lunch to work and ate it rather than buying something for a spontaneous kick. After the failed IVF in 2019, my energy levels plummeted further, and I opted out of life. My husband likes cooking but loathes the planning, so he ordered weekly meal kits. This temporary stopgap lasted for four and a half years and became an essential part of us not dying from scurvy. Technology supports our lives, and every time something new comes in, there's a chance that it will simplify another aspect so we can focus on things that only our brains can do.

MICHELLE, 41: I put in so many coping mechanisms before my diagnosis that it makes me look organised at work. I didn't know that everyone else didn't need them. For as long as I can remember, I've had a phone with a diary. Then, to stop getting distracted, I turned off all the pings and the envelopes you see on the corner of the screen when you've got emails. I made an auto folder for cc'd items so I don't get disturbed in my normal email because most are messages I don't need. My keys are on a lanyard because fifty times a day, I think, 'Have I lost my keys?' My poor work colleagues don't understand my incredibly complex filing system, but how would I find stuff if I didn't have separate files? It just doesn't compute. I never really had fidget toys, but I used to pick at my watch as a child and I'd bite my nails. Now, I constantly bite my lips. If it's not that, I've always got a hairband, or I twiddle the tabs on my umbrella or my bag. Those were all things that would keep me engaged to a degree, but I didn't realise that they helped the ADHD brain. My car keys always used to get lost. They now go on the fridge. The second I come in, the house keys go on the back of the door with the lanyard; the car key goes on the fridge. My boyfriend knows that when he comes around, he has to put them exactly where I would because I can put my keys down for half a second and lose them and the next day wonder where they are.

NAOMI, 26: I used to be very visual. I'd keep my things organised, but when it came to my thoughts and time, I was just a floating rock in space. I've done two pieces of homework in my entire life. I don't know how I wasn't caught out for it, maybe because I did okay at grades, but I would just completely forget that homework exists. I wouldn't plan. Revision was always last-minute. When I got to college, that was harder, and I would miss deadlines. I had no foresight or understanding of how to organise myself. When you're young, it's just school, but then it's things like work. Because planning is something that I will forget or not be able to do effectively, it's something that I had to learn. I'm still learning how to do it because it's hard AF. Cleaning is the best thing to procrastinate with. It's productive procrastinating, and you get a dopamine kick once everything's clean, but there's a thin line between getting overwhelmed and motivated. Because my head is so messy, I have to have less mess around me; otherwise I feel uncomfortable. My sister's always called me weird and a psycho because I like things being white and open, and it's because having space and cleanliness around me makes my brain feel less cluttered. I like to have an open wardrobe, or I'll forget what I have. If my clothes are arranged by colour and what I use regularly, it's easier for me to choose an outfit, and I like to use a hanging wardrobe so everything I need is at eye level.

ANDY, 52: Have you seen the episode of *Black Books* where Bernard Black's got to do his tax return? That's me every year. Fortunately, my sister-in-law is a chartered accountant. My brain goes into panic mode. I cannot get my head around adding up receipts. I would rather clean the toilet than do that, so now I do the Bernard Black thing where I get two handfuls of receipts out of my coat pockets, give them to my sister-in-law, and say, 'Turn that into a tax return, and here's money to do it,' so I don't even have to look at or think about it. It's fine; I know what I'm good at. Instead of struggling with doing my taxes and wondering what's wrong with me, I won't put myself through that stress. Almost all my receipts tend to be online. My email is my filing cabinet, so I'll create a smart mailbox bounded by a particular date and then do a search for 'receipt'. It's usually done in panic mode the day before I have to do it because only the adrenalin gets me to focus. There were many years when I was struggling financially, and I couldn't afford an accountant, and I'm lucky that I'm able to now.

AL, 41: A thing I find difficult as a woman with ADHD is when people say, 'But you're not hyperactive.' It's not about that; I can't go into a supermarket or get my head around how people do a weekly shop. I've got a chocolate orange in my fridge that somebody gave me in September last year, and I haven't eaten it because it's in the door, up high, and I've just completely forgotten it was there. Sometimes, I glance up and go, 'Oh, I've got a chocolate orange,' and then it will be another month until I remember. I want a glass-fronted fridge because it is like a magical mystery tour when I open it. I never have a clue what's in there. People don't think of it as causing issues because I'm quite outgoing and chatty, and I've got a lot of close friends, but I've lived in this flat for two years and haven't painted a single wall. I've got paint samples all over, decide on a colour, then change my mind, and never get it done. I lie in bed every night thinking, 'Right, tomorrow.' It just doesn't get done, and that's difficult because it means half-built bookcases behind me and books in piles all over the floor, affecting my social life. I've got friends that have never been round to visit, but because I'm not hyperactive and bouncing off the walls, people don't think it's a problem.

HANNAH, 50: I describe my brain as a goldfish bowl, and each thought is on an individually scrunched-up ball of paper. It's hard to get those individual thoughts out when I'm feeling overwhelmed; if my surroundings are disordered, it adds to that. I get a sense of pleasure from things being where they should be. Knowing what I'm doing and having lists and everything organised takes that pressure away. There's sometimes such an overload in my brain, so many thoughts and different stuff going on, that I need everything else to be organised. I guess it's about feeling I can have a sense of control. My home is really important to me. It's where I feel safe and I can be myself. I'm not super-super organised, but I need lists and everything on the calendar because otherwise, I forget. I've only recently realised that I have massive anxiety about being late, to the point where it gets distressing. Quite often, I turn up early. I can have my whole day mapped out with what I'm doing. My systems keep me safe, but I'm also responsible for two other little people, so it's not just about me; it's about looking after them and ensuring they're fed and picked up from school.

CLARE, 61: I was always late for school and jobs but would stay later and work all night on homework, revision and work projects. At home, I was chaotic, but I was fortunate to get a job with a very organised, strict, perfection-only studio manager who taught me excellent practice which I applied to every aspect of life. In my own homes, I would first make places for things, so energy went into putting up shelves, and building or buying cupboards and drawers and organising everything. I had an almost eidetic memory, and I still see and remember where things were from years ago.

ALICE, 40: I never had the right books at school, had my homework done or was in the right place at the right time. This was always perceived to have been done with intention, but it wasn't. I am a people pleaser and would have loved to have been 'good', but it wasn't possible. I was endlessly punished, and no one thought to help me become more organised, because they believed me to be intelligent and, therefore, capable, so I was branded 'lazy' and have over-compensated ever since. My parents' nickname for me was 'Slapdash Alice'. I also have no sense of direction and can't find my way anywhere because I'm never paying attention. On the extremely rare occasion that I'm going somewhere I don't need a GPS to find, I still have to turn it on. I will miss turns even when I know the way because I'm thinking about something else. My life is a series of unfinished projects. I never get to the finish line of anything without something more exciting luring me away. Phone alarms with labels have changed my life. I have between fifteen and twenty going off every day. They remind me about work things, children's drop-offs and pick-ups, things that need to go in or out of ovens ... I don't understand how people like me survived before this invention. Without them, I can think that I need to remember to do something in five minutes and then never think about that again until my house catches fire or a school calls me.

JAMES, 47: One of the ADHD accounts I follow on Twitter had a brilliant post saying, 'ADHD is like turning up for work and realising you've left your calendar on shuffle.' That is 100 per cent it. I have a list of things to do and just do things on a whim. I'll start this and stop that, then go off and do that and then do this, and it's just fucking carnage. Without organisation, nothing would get done. I have a loose to-do list – I used to use my inbox to do this; that was a terrible idea – and I triage that by what interests me at any given moment. I will try and do urgent things first because they need to be done, but with everything else, it's just whatever interests me then, which is frustrating for many of the people I work with because I'm like, 'Oh, this thing's interesting. Nobody cares about that, but I'm going to do it!'

When I was a teenager, I always said, 'Ask me on Saturday morning because I don't know what I'll want to do till then.' My plans are almost always made on the day or the day before. I don't like to lock myself down because I don't know if that's what I want to do or if I'll be in the right headspace. I like to be spontaneous and say, let's go into London and go on the London Eye. Fuck it, let's do it. Let's go on holiday at the weekend. That sounds slightly manic, but it's just that I like to have that flexibility.

I'm good with money, organisation and basic life admin because I have a routine and a schedule. I have time on the weekend to sit down with my many lever arch files. I use accounts programs, and I balance my money. I'm very fastidious with that stuff, so it doesn't get away from me. I use a reminder app called Due, which is amazing because it nags you, and that is the crucial difference from all the others. It will ping every minute until I acknowledge it, and that's what I need. Otherwise, I'll remember it, and it will be gone out of my head five seconds later. I use this for everything I do for work – picking up my child, taking out the bins, you name it. It has been the most life-changing of all the things I've used.

I'm not obsessive-compulsive tidy, but I find that, because my brain is chaotic, I need my environment to be calming or it's too much. My mum was always tidy, so it was easy enough for me to learn. I've got to the point where if I have multiple paperbacks in a series and then a hardback, I have to rebuy the book as a paperback so that they fit in the same place because separating a series will fuck my whole filing system, and I can't have it.

SEAN, 38: Three months ago, I found out I was pre-diabetic. I can still turn it around, which I'm doing. The NHS said they could refer me for three months free at the local gym because of my BMI, where they'll do a load of tests and weigh me on my first and last day. Perfect! That's enough accountability. I don't really mind being bigger; I'm not bothered about losing weight, but I would like not to be diabetic. This all came about because I was getting migraines, which turned out to be caused by blood pressure related to weight and eating entire packs of biscuits every other evening – turns out, that's not good for you. I was so up for it, but I missed the phone call and got an email asking me to call them. I haven't contacted them since because the pressure's gone. If they sent another email going, 'This runs out soon, get in touch with us,' that'd probably do the trick. And I hate that that is so obvious, yet I'm doing nothing about it. I know exactly what would motivate me to do it, and I know I should do it regardless, but I won't, which aggravates me. For all the progress I've made in situations like this, this is just unnecessary.

THE PROFESSIONAL VIEW

JENN JORDAN (@orjenise) works between Yorkshire and London as a professional organiser. She declutters, unpacks, puts systems in place in homes, and has specific training in working with clients with ADHD and hoarding disorder.

I get clients saying, 'I just wish someone would come and burn my house down.' I absolutely know how that feels. When I'm stressed, I'm straight back out there, staring at stuff. Even though I've become this tidy person, it's still who I am, and I have to be careful when I'm stressed and tired. Somebody tried to break into my house last week, and I spent 380 quid on jumpers. I know. Even better, they sent me the wrong one, which says 'Future MILF'.

When I started this business officially about five years ago, ADHD wasn't on my radar. Just not a thing. Whereas the number of women my age now where someone's said, 'Your kid's got ADHD,' and they go, 'That sounds like me,' and then, 'Oh! I've got it too,' is massive. Many people's reaction to being unorganised is to completely over-organise themselves. I have two categories: stuff for charity and stuff for the bin or recycling. To someone else, there are seventeen: the metal bag, the electric bag, a battery bag . . . Just, 'Oh right, that's how we've got completely out of control here.' I don't make any changes for people with ADHD; it's not like, 'I'm working with someone with ADHD today, so I'll do everything differently.' It's all the same: big categories, labels, working out how it will work for you, and then ideally going back to see what is and isn't working so you can tweak it. Don't think, 'I've got ADHD, I can't be organised, and there's no point in me trying.' Everyone needs to tweak things. It might not be working, not because you've got ADHD; it might just not work for you. In everybody's house, however chaotic they've been, some things are working for them.

I'm not doing anything you'd never work out yourself, but 'put that there and then I'll be able to find it' was a revelation to me, as it is to many other people. I used to be untidy. This has been a skill I've taught myself and got better at. For context, my dad bought and sold antiques, so we were always at auctions, and I've grown up with lots of stuff. I love all of that. I love looking at stuff as much as possible. I was out every weekend just buying, buying, buying. That little boost gives you a little 'Ooh!', but eventually, the opposite starts happening. People think being organised is doing a lot of work at *The Home Edit* level. The way I do it is much lazier. I don't want to spend my time looking for things and putting things away; like I always used to lose the TV remote – there's a tray on the table for it now. You're not shouting at your kids: 'Where's that?' because it's there, and if it's not there, it's their fault. I can put all these systems in place, but I can't force your husband to put the tools back in the toolbox.

I'm sure you brush your teeth every morning, however unorganised you feel. Your toothpaste is there. Your toothbrush is there. The floss is there. The mouthwash is there. It works because it's where it needs to be. That is really what we're doing all over the house. All the good brands are at eye level at the supermarket because they pay top whack for that. That's where you want all your useful stuff: plates, glasses, etc. Everything you don't use very often, your slow cooker and the popcorn maker, can go down on the budget shelves at the bottom. If I open a cupboard, I want to see what's there. Labels are good for that, obviously, and I like those big tubs with a lowered bit at the front so you can see what's inside, then when you've got something in your hand – oh, it goes in there. Even if it's in the wrong place, in two seconds, it's in the right place again. Kitchens can get unwieldy quickly; if you can't find your spices, you will buy four more of the same thing.

One big thing people do is put things in boxes with lids on. It might as well be invisible. Lids are barriers. Even something in front of a book on a bookshelf might stop you from reading it. Be aware of barriers, although you can also use them in your favour. My vitamins were next to the toothbrush – it didn't work, and I never remembered to take them. Now I have to pick them up to get to the cereal – it's in my hand. I've got to take these – and I take them every day.

People think of decluttering (and I suppose I'm part of this problem) as this big transformation. I don't want people doing hours and hours. You want to be taking little bites constantly. Get rid of your cardboard boxes. When you buy a plastic bag in the supermarket, think, 'Next time, I must remember to take a plastic bag because I've got sixty-eight at home, and they start to take up quite a lot of space!' In January and September, I try to use up a hundred things a month. Gather all your toiletries and see what needs to be used. Day two is food. Some people hit a hundred on just those two: gifts, little samples and stuff from hotel rooms, the thing you forgot you bought at John Lewis last week. Suddenly, you've got this massive box with two hundred pounds' worth of toiletries that you've completely forgotten you owned.

Be careful about what comes in and learn to say no. If you're really into the sales, stand for an extra two minutes and work out the likelihood that you will wear lime green. Keep analysing what's not working for you. Why are you not wearing that top? Why are you putting it back in the wardrobe with a big sigh? It's never going to be right; let it go. Don't wear the old tatty thing covered in hair dye to sleep in; maybe you could just buy a nice thing. I'm always trying to buy one good thing. I'd rather have one good shower gel than a gift set.

Cheatsheet: How to build an ADHD-friendly routine

Start the day with a boost. If bribing yourself with the prospect of a delicious coffee gets you to go for a walk, do it. A morning ping of achievement and a task accomplished gets you off on the right foot.

Anchor your habits. Attach anything you want to do regularly to something you already do. Link taking your meds to brushing your teeth, or going to bed to putting your phone downstairs, having a bath and putting your good pyjamas on. BJ Fogg and James Clear have lovely books on creating habits that stick.

Choose shelves over cupboards. Remove doors if it's helpful to do so and if they aren't above the stove. I am that basic bitch who puts things in labelled jars. They don't need to be, but doing that gives me pleasure, so I use them rather than going to the shop to buy junk.

Prioritise eye level. Put anything that you want reminders to eat at the top of the fridge door. Sauces and longer-life stuff can go in the crisper drawer if you have one, aka The Place Vegetables Go to Be Forgotten.

Consider apps and hardware. Due and Sweepy can be excellent to externalise household chores and reduce emotional load or guilt. A smartwatch or home assistant (such as Alexa or Google Home) can be similarly helpful for keeping timers and dates to hand with audible reminders. Put your hyperfocus to good use and find them second-hand for a better deal.

When I was younger, I would get a second wind at ten o'clock and be wide awake. I have to make sure I get to bed before a certain time, with earplugs so I'm not distracted by noise, and I have a sleep mask if needed. I'll jot down any thoughts on my phone to get them out of my head. And something my therapist told me to do when I'm lying there worrying is to ask myself, what can I do about this right now?

– HANNAH, 50

My daily to-do list is accompanied by a little column that says 'to-be' to remind me this is who I am, and I'm not defined by what I do. To be happy, kind, considerate and patient. Not just 'to-do'.

– DR TONY LLOYD

CHAPTER NINE

Self-esteem

One spring, a therapist asked me to focus on a single cherry tree in blossom – I'd said I felt like I needed an entire street of them to feel anything at all. The idea of finding joy can seem revoltingly twee and whimsical, but as navigating life becomes more complex it arguably becomes more important. My capacity for joy is still there, even if the well runs very dry. Paying attention to tiny things helps, an aspect of mindfulness I never understood. I always thought it had something to do with concentrating for long periods, which is why, every year, I get a reminder from Be Mindful telling me balefully that it's five years since I completed week one. I saw a lovely trend on TikTok about romanticising your life, almost imagining you're in the opening song from *Beauty and the Beast*, and it makes even the most mundane parts of life feel nicer and more unique. Those tiny moments of awareness have the same effect that writing a gratitude list does, opening your eyes to elements of it so that you can keep grounded in what's happening here, now, rather than being drawn away on the current of what is happening around you.

Acceptance is such a massive part of it and an ongoing learning curve. We've spent years trying to fit into somebody else's box, particularly in the UK, a box that has a poor understanding of mental health, let alone neurological conditions. Some experience this as compartmentalisation rather than just being one person. I have periods where I feel like an avatar in a meat suit, my mind and body completely separate rather than one unit charging through life. To pass as a human being, I had to achieve more than anyone else because I couldn't guarantee that I knew how to behave correctly or what might get a strange reaction and lead me to think, 'Shit, I've done something wrong.' I can feel that I almost don't exist, that I'm a balloon made up of other people's opinions of me. It's horrible to walk around feeling as though you are a giant monster hidden under a sheet, and at any moment, that sheet could come off, and people see who you truly are.

The title of Kate Kelly and Peggy Ramundo's book *You Mean I'm Not Lazy, Stupid or Crazy?!* resonates so strongly with me because of that bewilderment about why I'm not doing things that regular people seem to manage. I'm not making this phone call or I'm not sending this email. Why aren't I doing the physio? I physically can't get the pilot light going. I don't have the techniques, so

I must wait until my brain decides, 'Oh, right. I'm just going to light it spontaneously, and we'll do it now at two o'clock in the morning.'

It's hard to have self-esteem when you don't feel aligned with yourself.

We can't fully accept something when we can't articulate what's happening. It's always difficult being at the forefront of something that is misunderstood. Even if you're reasonably robust, having people not quite believe it and, by extension, in you – that can chip away at you. I regularly dream about school and people I have not seen nor thought about for decades, as though I want them to know I am well adjusted. It wasn't my fault I was like that. I want a do-over so that they will think better of me. When I wake up, I get that chance with the people in my life now.

SEAN, 38: This is not a fun thing to admit. When I was with my then-girlfriend, now wife, I had what I later learned was an emotional affair. Not to use the ADHD as an excuse because it's not. It was like, 'Oh, this is new and interesting!' Through going to therapy, I discovered I had no tools for dealing with affection. I didn't know how to turn it away because I'd never had to, and because it was new and interesting, I jeopardised my relationship. I remember a couple of sessions in, the therapist was like, 'How would you describe yourself?' It was as though someone had stolen my voice. I'm whatever I need to be, depending on what room I'm in and who's there, and it was like, 'Oh God, that's a real problem because if that's all you do, you're just being dragged around by other people's expectations.' I worked through that. I am grateful to have understood it, but it would have been nice to have caught that earlier. Happily, I've not had the slightest inclination since because it was through that understanding that I got to define who I am. It's not a case of, 'People need this from me now, so I guess I'll do and say this.' That was a valuable experience and a big lesson in self-esteem, but how it came about does not feel great.

CLEMENTINE, 36: My father and I have always been extremely close, like best friends. He's not very well now, but a few years ago, he said to me, 'Clem,' – and he loves me so much. I know he does – 'I just find it amazing, incredible, that you've got good academic marks at university, and you own your own business.' I said, 'Why is that incredible?' He said, 'I just didn't think you'd come to anything.' And he didn't mean it in a bad way. He didn't. He adores me; I know that. He knew I'd grow up with good morals; but as for having a career, getting myself organised, he just couldn't see how I would ever find a way to do that. I find this really poignant and feel very much like I let my Dad down in giving him so much to worry about when I was a child.

My default position at the moment is: this is who I am. I don't know how not to be. I just am. If I like someone and am comfortable with someone, I will just talk to them. I don't really care what they think of me. There are times when I'm embarrassed by being ADHD and the traits that come with it, and then I feel defensive because I realise, 'No, I'm not an idiot. I can do things really well.' I was diagnosed when I was thirty-five. It's painful that people judged me and got me completely wrong for so many years. I might as well have had a different name and identity, and I had no idea. I always found it confusing. 'Why am I such an idiot? Why am I always late? Why didn't I hear that piece of information? Why can't I find that pen? Why do I find religious education lessons so boring that I would literally rather go and watch paint dry?' I'd agonise over these things, why why why? I came to the conclusion it was because I'm a bit crap. It does make me sad sometimes to think back. I want to go back in time and say, 'Clem, you're not crap. You're really quite marvellous. It's just life's tricky for you.' In a way, having my children, who have both now been diagnosed with ADHD, is like a self-indulgent opportunity for me to rectify everything that went wrong with me. I'm ferociously protective of them being allowed to be who they are without judgement and making sure that they grow up knowing that they have ADHD, that some things are really hard, some things are boring – some people are boring! – and that's absolutely fine because they're brilliant. I think so far I've achieved that.

EMILY, 48: I am the worst kind of ADHDer in some ways, in that I'm never late, I'm on top of everything, and I have eight bazillion lists. If anything falls, it's my sense of self-worth. Externally, I always delivered to such a high fucking standard. Even when I had postnatal depression and psychosis, my psychs were like, 'Your level of functioning is so high that it's normal people's low. It's just obscene that you can do this.' I think that's because I'm so tightly coiled mentally. I've had to compensate for so much of my life that I've trained myself into that high level of function, so when my executive function falls apart, it really falls apart. In my friendship groups, I am the person that often keeps the groups together. I'm the one that's like, 'Let's go do something,' or, 'I haven't seen you for a long time.' I'll always be the first one to reach out, and there have been times when the RSD of that is also like, 'Why doesn't anyone reach out to me?' And they don't because I've fucking trained them not to because they all know that I will!

Two things from the immense therapy journey that I've been on is that I spent forty-two years believing things about me that are quite negative and not true, and I do not want to spend the next forty years of my life still believing them. I felt like I was given a gift, as much as I paid for it. The cost of getting there was difficult, but how often are we given time to examine what we truly believe about ourselves and change it? One of my favourite therapists was this woman who looked like the designer from *The*

Incredibles. She was just hysterical. Her favourite saying was 'ABC', Awareness Before Change. That has been one of the best therapeutic principles for me. You don't know what you don't know, but now I do, what do I want to do about it? The knowing is everything. If someone doesn't return a text and I've decided that they hate me and are probably moving countries right now because they couldn't wait to get away – I can stop and be like, *Is that really happening?* Or do you feel a bit bruised that you're the one who starts that conversation a lot of the time? But if you look back at the messages, you're not the only one, so maybe that person is busy right now. Or maybe they are a dick, but is that why they're not responding to the message you sent two hours ago?

The other big thing is, 'Will this still bother me in a few days? Is it going to bother me in three months? Will I even care?' But again, if those things had happened and I didn't know it was ADHD, I would assume that I was the problem. What the diagnosis gifts me is that there isn't a problem. That's just how my brain works, and that's only a problem if I decide it is. There's great power in that.

NAOMI, 26: What's helped is learning about myself and knowing it's a disability. I feel less saddened by the fact that people may not understand something and more encouraged to speak up. Not everybody will understand it, the same way that some men will pretend that women have 'women's issues'. Community is important because you need to know you're not the only person going through that. Otherwise, you will make yourself the problem because your brain is looking for a solution: 'Why is this the problem? Well, I'm the one who keeps doing it, so I'm the problem.' If you have lots of people, then you don't feel that way. And also, have the biggest grace with yourself. Don't be a meanie panini to yourself, basically.

JAMES, 47: At school, I would sit down, the lesson would start, they'd have me for two or three minutes, and then I would daydream. That was my entire school career. My grades were Cs and Ds during the year, but I'd get As and Bs in my exams because I could focus and get it done. No one understood why; it didn't make any sense to them, so I was branded as lazy. 'He's a dreamer', 'He seems a very bright boy, but he doesn't apply himself'; all of these things that we all get, and so I carried that with me to adulthood. 'I am a lazy person who doesn't apply myself' – that was a label I gave myself, and I believed that until alarmingly recently when my former boss stopped me and said, 'You are not lazy.' I was a bit taken aback by it. I never thought I was particularly bright till a colleague turned to me ten years ago and expressed admiration. It really floored me because that was not my self-image at all. I saw myself as someone who struggled. It wasn't until I started to realise that it's just the way my brain works, that it's not stupidity. In the same way as with any learning disability, it's an obstacle that makes things difficult for me that for other people are very easy, but intelligence has nothing to do with it.

The damage from school stuff was limited because my mum's acutely dyslexic, so she had infinite patience with me. She never criticised; she was always wonderful about everything. Because she had such an abusive time at school, where she was literally beaten in front of the class for not being able to spell things, she was incredibly understanding, and she never had a go at me for any of it. It was only the self-image things I took with me; I don't think I had a lot of deep-rooted trauma.

I always did well in exams because I could revise and teach myself. My GCSE results were okay; they weren't outstanding. Same with my A level results; they were decent. I got a 2:1 degree; it was fine. It got me to the point of being able to do it myself when I could be arsed. A friend who recently discovered she has ADHD is not necessarily as happy about it because she sees missed opportunities and unfulfilled potential, which frustrates her. I got my dream job and have been there for a long time. It's not perfect – let's not pretend it is – but I got that, so I don't have that much to complain about.

Having the awareness and therapy has made me understand why I struggle and has helped me compensate. It's also helped me understand why people don't see things the same way I do. When I originally went out into the workforce, Mum said, 'You just get a job; it doesn't matter where.' I was doing a menial job at the time, and I remember saying, 'I genuinely would kill myself if this were my life,' and she said, 'You're just being dramatic.' I said, 'I'm not, but I don't know how to make you understand that.'

And what she can't understand is, for my brain, the thought of spending all day doing something that bored me was the kind of torture that you possibly would take a long walk off a short pier to get out of. I needed to find something that stimulated me, that I enjoyed, and loved doing. And I got that! So that in itself is what's carried me along thus far.

HANNAH, 50: When I'm being hard on myself, I think, 'What would you say, Hannah, if your client said this to you?' I have to talk to myself. I'm a perfectionist, and it's crippling sometimes, everything having to be right. I can't just type out an essay; I have to master it because I don't want to get it wrong. I don't want people to think I'm stupid. I don't want to think I'm stupid. I am an overthinker. That's part of who I am; I recognise it as part of my ADHD. Sometimes, it can be disruptive, but thinking makes me an excellent counsellor because I think about my clients. I think about all sorts of things. I question myself and what I'm doing. If I make a decision now, I've thought it through. I didn't trust myself when I was younger. I didn't trust that I would make the right decision; but having had lots of therapy and counselling training, I do now. I know it's the right decision for me if I make it. Overthinking is being thoughtful. Thoughtful is being caring. Caring about what others think can be reframed into thinking of others and what others want or need. But it is also remembering that I'm not central to everything. I can't be responsible for everything. I'm a small cog.

What's changed is my sense of self-acceptance. There's nothing wrong with me; ADHD is part of my identity, and even though it makes life more difficult, I like having it. When I'm feeling scatty and I can't remember stuff, I remind myself, 'You've got ADHD, you've got dyslexia; this is why you find it difficult.' It gives me more confidence and self-belief. If I find an essay hard, I can tell myself, 'No, you are intelligent. You are capable.' I'm more confident in myself and more accepting of other people.

THE PROFESSIONAL VIEW

Shahroo Izadi is a behavioural change specialist who developed her skills working across the addiction and recovery sector and through her own experience of binge eating. She has written two bestselling books: The Kindness Method and The Last Diet.

When building a habit, the cumulative effects component is essential. Zoom out and ask yourself what the impact will be on the things that matter to you if you do something for, say, ten days. People tell me things like waking up in the morning less irritable, more inclined to go for a walk and less inclined to yell at their partner.

These are the important things, not, 'Did you know that if you sleep half an hour earlier, you are decreasing the likelihood of getting blah?' It doesn't matter if it's a spreadsheet or a piece of laundry. It becomes an identity piece: 'I want to be the sort of person who does what they said they would do.' Take the outcome of a task out of the equation and find pride in doing what you said you would do. Draw self-esteem from saying, 'I'm watching, and that matters.' That witnessing component is important with ADHD. If I go to a co-working space, I will work harder because people will witness me, and I don't want them to see me getting up. I give my clients permission to work on the things they care about and help them to care about their own opinion of themselves.

From an evolutionary perspective, we are wired to be anxious and attuned to our threats and deficits. It's on you to bring the good stuff to the forefront of your mind, which can feel a bit intangible, so, in black and white, write it down and give yourself the evidence. If a person described that you were kind, what might they say you were doing physically? When you see it written down, you go, 'Oh, yeah, that's the picture of an all right person.' Sometimes, I'll have to look in a notebook to see that I'm successful. It's extraordinary how many days I'll think I'm not because everything seems to be going wrong. We can also see that black-and-white splitting thinking in borderline personality disorder. The younger girls I work with do it a lot, and they become very aware of it.

One helpful thing is to say there was never any expectation to be perfect in the first place. When I think about why I love my friends, many of them do things that I find annoying, and the same with me. I worked through those before knowing that they were ADHD symptoms, and I had started to own them. A great way of doing this is getting on board with what you're good at and what you like about yourself. I'm loyal and present when I am with someone. What are you non-negotiably great at? When you have accepted what those things are, you can ask yourself, 'What are the things I'm not great at?' If you go on to work on them, fine, but do your work on understanding that you're worthy of being just as flawed as everyone else. Find people who love that part of you and don't see it as a downside. Remedying those things is not a criterion to be accepted or loved or for people to want to be around you. People do things I find annoying all the bloody time. That doesn't mean I'm writing them off.

DR TONY LLOYD: What gives somebody self-esteem? It is that relationship-driven genetic imperative, that sense that you belong to a social group, are valued, and can make a meaningful contribution. The universal design is such that diversity is integral to our evolution, in the same way that biodiversity is integral to the planet. In a rapidly changing technology-driven world and culture, it's only now that those who think differently are being valued and seen, reclaiming their right to be here and belong when they've experienced years of systemic prejudice and exclusion. It requires a certain amount of self-esteem to say, 'Hang on, I deserve better.'

Labels help us organise things, but some labels are value-laden and deficit-based. What does it feel like walking around with that unless you've been able to reframe it for yourself? There's something quite empowering there. What is this instinctive drive that makes you think, 'I am not going to be kept down; I am going to self-actualise; I am going to achieve something. It might not be something someone else values, but it has to have meaning. If it doesn't, I'll never have self-esteem because I'll constantly value myself by others' standards.' Seeing so many people with ADHD thrive and fight back inspires me. That's the human spirit. Trying to be alive and not just some soulless empty construct that thinks this is what people do. Well, actually – is that what people need?

Self-esteem and self-confidence are two sides of the same coin, but they're not necessarily the same thing. With low self-esteem, you often have this unconscious instinct to protect your self-concept as being lovable, belonging and valued. I had a lot of good friends who gave me a sense of belonging. My crisis of identity came from being a psychiatric patient. I spent six months in hospital when I was fifteen. I never told anybody what happened to me. My friends were told I'd fallen over, banged my head and lost my memory because somebody had come in to see me when I had burn marks on my temples.

I was hyperactive and depressed, and of course, that didn't make sense in those days, so they gave me six sessions of electroconvulsive shock treatments and filled me with psychotropics. I was in a ward for adult men with short-stay drink problems. You think, 'What am I doing here?' Little did I know they were some of the kindest people. They used to come in and visit me when they left. The psychiatrists and nurses were amazingly kind. Some of them used to take me home for the weekend so I didn't get institutionalised. Their kindness, rather than their treatment, is what helped me survive.

I was in care for a few months and then put in a flat at sixteen. I couldn't boil an egg. When I look back, I don't know how I survived. There was that pervasive level of anxiety that children with ADHD experience, and I was also a gay man, although I wasn't quite aware of that then, so I learned how to pretend to be confident. I had good social and friendship skills, but there was always a bit of me pretending to be something that I thought was me and maybe was me, but I never knew if I had the confidence to believe it.

Cheatsheet: How to deal with ADHD-related shame

First, do something. Rumination comes from the brain's Default Mode Network (sometimes nicknamed the 'demon'). Break out of it by dancing, singing a song, stepping through a doorway or counting down out loud.

Practise self-acceptance. This doesn't mean self-care, self-love or mantras. It means accepting yourself – all of yourself – and being gentle with the good and the bad. ACT, DBT and CBT are valuable forms of psychotherapy to try, backed up with positive self-talk.

Do esteemable things. Show up. Help others. Respect others and yourself.

Do the next right thing. This is actually the title of a song from Frozen 2, but God, it applies to so much in life.

Get to know yourself. How do you respond to certain things? How does stress show up in your body? Appreciate what you need, and prioritise that.

Practise gratitude. This does not mean self-flagellating generalisations like, 'I'm grateful that I'm not a Victorian chimney sweep and that I have somewhere to live.' Write down very specific things that you are thankful for from the day you are writing: 'My coffee was nice this morning. I got my favourite seat on the bus. My child slept in half an hour later than usual. I had a chat with our postman.' This helps you to slow down and to observe the world and that you are part of it.

Join a research study. Be part of the solution. ADHD developments need research, and men have been less likely to sign up. If you're male, break this trend! Good places to start are adhdresearchlab.com, ukaan.org, edgiuk.org and gladstudy.org.uk.

> What has really helped is learning how I feel when I am losing control or feeling overwhelmed and then listening to my body and removing myself from the situation.
>
> **– ANSHUL, 27**

CHAPTER TEN

Money

I have no excuse for how appalling I have been with my finances. To say I am privileged is a colossal understatement. My parents paid for my education, gave me an allowance and copped the bill for my postgrad. They bailed me out through my twenties. I've lost count of how often my dad paid off my credit card bill. When I finally came to my senses and broke up with a dreadful boyfriend I'd lent four hundred pounds to, my mum both gave me the money (I repaid it years later, a tiny brick in the wall) and bought me a ticket to Glastonbury to celebrate being shot of him. I was an albatross around my family's neck for far longer than was appropriate, dignified or necessary. My industry isn't well paid, but it's not an excuse. I had an incredible level of support and flailed around being useless. Living within my means was a concept I couldn't grasp. I tried to budget, doing my sums on paper and allocating money for rent and groceries, but it never stuck. When

I ran out, I'd use my credit card or borrow from the next month. I wasn't buying snazzy tech or designer outfits – clothes often came from eBay, which was a massive dopamine hit – but I was absolutely failing as an adult. Seeing my friends manage made me feel utterly ashamed. I felt like I was scrabbling on ice to even think about mid-term concepts like budgeting, let alone long-term ones like saving. Immediacy was the only thing I understood. One friend saved up fifty pounds a month for years to take a group of us to London's oldest restaurant, Rules, for her twenty-fifth birthday. I couldn't plan for next Tuesday.

My bank account was an ongoing firefight; my savings account was there in name only. Any savings I managed to build would go out the next month to pay off my credit card or wrest my daily account out of overdraft. I pored over the MoneySavingExpert website, amazed at how people got themselves out of enormous debt or improved their credit rating. I was utterly unable to see how I could achieve the same. The classic trick of moving credit card balances around to take advantage of interest-free periods simply resulted in me racking up more debt, now on multiple cards, which would be bumped up by fines, interest or forgetting to pay bills.

I would have continued rolling along in the same disastrous way if it hadn't been for my getting better paid work, and technological improvement; in parity with Professor Young's observation that ADHD treatment can't work before acceptance, I realised that I couldn't start saving until I sorted out the rest of my finances. Everything went online – if paper bills were involved, they might as well not exist. My credit card went into the attic – there was no point getting purchase protection if I kept forgetting I'd made the purchases in the first place. I moved my banking to Monzo so that it was on my phone, and subscribed to the business account, which automatically took a percentage off each payment and put it into a pot for tax. If I took on regular contracts, I subscribed to the You Need A Budget app, which I found entirely addictive for allocating money to digital envelopes for everything from app subscriptions to haircuts and bills and forcing me to be realistic about where my money was going because, like my alcohol and food habits, money was something that I couldn't look at without feeling physically sick.

When I did examine my finances, I saw how much I frittered money, just as I would nibble away at snacks and binge foods rather than eating proper meals. I had a scarcity mindset that meant I always felt too poor (and I was not poor) for a holiday, an adequate grocery shop or other significant purchases, which just meant lots of little bits of shopping that gave me a lovely boost but emptied my account at a startling rate. Financial coach Clare Seal highlights a 2022 survey by Monzo and YouGov which found that living with ADHD can cost an extra £1,600 a year because of money management difficulties. People with ADHD were three times more likely than people without to miss bill payments and twice as likely to experience finance-related anxiety. As well as fines from organisational disasters, I felt an impulse to spend money on the magic button to make me feel better or to try something that might fix my brain. I have spent thousands on various treatments and therapies, which helped a little but couldn't treat the Big Boss problem because we didn't know it was there. The 'ADHD tax' can also have knock-on effects on daily life. I was once too embarrassed to ask my then-boyfriend for the twenty-five pounds it would cost to get the morning-after pill on a Sunday, so I went to the GUM clinic the following day, where I had a wildly painful IUD fitted instead. It didn't occur to me that this was our, not my, responsibility, just that I was stupid, and this was my fault.

Dr Ned Hallowell talks about lifestyle factors being as big an area of ADHD treatment as meds, therapy and coaching. Specifically, he highlights having a suitable job and a suitable partner. If you have either or both, your stress levels will be lower and you will require less stimulation through shopping, spending or other dopamine raisers. Crucially, you will be in an environment that supports you and empowers change. My tech-focused husband has improved my attitude to finances in ways I never imagined. He showed me Monzo, and having my accounts visible in one app

– even the non-Monzo ones – has been incredible. The Coin Jar function that rounds up purchases to the pound and puts the extra in a pot means I build up little savings without realising it. We share a joint account for bills and its Coin Jar goes to a pot for renovations. I can separate work, personal and joint costs and identify where money needs to be while swiping between them in one place. I feel like a duckling in my finance lessons, but at least I'm finally in the right pond.

AL, 41: I'm incredibly lucky to be able to afford this apartment. My mum died when I was sixteen, so I had some inheritance. It was left until I was supposedly grown up enough to deal with it, but my credit rating was shot to pieces, so I'm on an adverse credit-type mortgage. I'm constantly in debt. I am really fortunate that my parents have always been able to bail me out. I was twenty when I went to rehab and came out the day before I turned twenty-one. My parents had already bailed me out to the tune of about a hundred thousand pounds, and that had nothing to do with university or student loans; that was blowing money. I still don't have a great understanding of it. I can write a budget, and it looks great, but it may as well be in Japanese for all the good it does, and that's really difficult as a forty-one-year-old.

My dad phoned me today and asked, 'How are you? Is your mortgage up?' No, I've got three more years on it, so that's okay. He said, 'How are your finances?' I didn't want to tell him I'm thirty grand in debt because I shouldn't be asking my seventy-five-year-old father to bail me out. I know he would without even blinking, but you get to that stage where you're like, 'I've just got to get a grip on it.' I'm fortunate that my credit rating now is excellent – it was less than a hundred when I got this flat – but the spending doesn't stop. I look at my emails in the morning, and I've woken up in the middle of the night and been buying things because I couldn't sleep. Parcels turn up, and I'm like, 'Ooh, what's this?'

My mum was the same. She was two hundred thousand pounds in debt when she died. She'd hidden it from everybody. If I had a bad day at school, she'd always say, 'Let's go shopping.' Some is learned behaviour, but it's a bit more than that. It's all tied together, isn't it, food and money? It feels insurmountable at times. But I'm lucky. I'm in a stable job, and somehow, I've repaired my credit rating, but I need to work on the shopping and the spending.

I think because I've never felt very self-confident if someone's asked me to do something, even if I can't afford it, I will do it because that invite might not come again. I used to show people love through gifts, which Mum did. It's recognising that I'm in my forties now. I don't need to buy people extravagant gifts. I've got friends that have been in my life for twenty-one-plus years. They're not going anywhere. They're not sticking around just because I'm extravagant. That's not why they're here.

JAMES, 47: My mum was a single mother. She never earned very much; by the month's end, we were running on fumes. She drilled into me from an early age that you keep every bank statement, you keep a folder, and when you get a bank statement, you go through every line, making sure you know what it is and that it's supposed to be there and you balance your books. Since I left home, I have kept spreadsheets – I use a piece of software now – and I go through every statement line by line when I get it and ensure that every expense is where it should be. It's just habit, all of this stuff, and having the impetus to do it. My mum was so hot on it, and it's always stayed with me that this is important, and then you work it into your routine because often routines are the master of this. If you get into a routine, it becomes second nature. I might be listening to a podcast while I'm doing it, but I do it.

CLARE, 42: When you've got £30k of debt, you've partied far too hard, you've not hit your true potential, you've found yourself unable to action a task as you can't do it, you've been told off for being too much, your head has 395 tabs running at once and you've had a lifetime of this, then you know what it's like to be me and trust me, that's not how most people live. I could have done more career-wise and job-wise. I went to uni but didn't finish my second year because I was out clubbing all weekend and missing sleep. I went into retail, then the call centre for a bank, and then

I worked in financial services doing admin. I could have stayed somewhere and had a career, built myself up, not got to forty still earning twenty thousand. I should have been on forty thousand a year or above like my friends. Instead, I've got thirty grand's worth of debt, and a lot of that is from impulsivity. In January, I decided I liked Funko Pops. By the end of February, I had about twenty. Why? I'm forty-two years old. I don't need to do that.

The medication has helped; I'm on Elvanse, although my psychiatrist says my impulsivity scores are still through the roof. I have a ridiculous amount of clothes. When I'm feeling bad, I book a holiday. It's all gone on the credit card. It's been a consistent thing, loans, credit cards . . . Other people have savings accounts; I've got none of that because I've just spent it. I put something on a credit card because I don't want to say no to going out and having fun, buying something, going somewhere or getting a tattoo. I still have no sense of a way to save up for it – I need it now.

BETHAN, 42: The money I have wasted on being unable to pay fines on time: I am keeping London going with my ULEZ charges. There was a period when the auto pay wasn't working, so you had to go in and do it manually. I can't do that within the timeframe. I've spent, honestly, hundreds on it. I had to start putting them through my business account because it is a work expense now. I am driving to a meeting and have forgotten to do it. It's a nightmare. I also mitigate my sloth days by walking fifteen minutes to a deli to get an overpriced coffee. It's ridiculous and wasteful, but I am getting out of the house, and that's my carrot.

MICHELLE, 41: My dad always drilled into me that you should have at least three months' money in the bank to get by if your job ever went. My friends joke that I've had a pension since I was eighteen. I can only ensure that my money is where it's supposed to be by having multiple bank accounts. One bank has my ISA, mortgage account and savings account. The other is with Starling, who has these money pots, so you just put money into stuff you might want for a rainy day. I wrote to my main bank that I prefer to use a different account for everyday usage because they didn't have pots. They came back and said, 'What do you mean? Why would you need all that stuff?' I'm like, 'You don't understand my brain. That's fine. But without the ability to save for different things at different times, I will find myself saving for something and then using it for something I shouldn't.' I have a car pot. I have a hair pot. Whenever I need a haircut, I take money from there and put in twenty, forty pounds a month – sorted. Trapeze? I have an expensive hobby, so I have to save up for it all year round to pay for it in one go. I couldn't have this life if I didn't have that level of organisation.

Once a year, I'll sit down with my spreadsheet and look at my current financial situation, incomings and outgoings, mortgage, car, whatever it is. I need to ensure I've got that amount of money going from my account on the day I get paid. It has to be then, down to the point where if I know I will be paid early at Christmas, that direct debit date is changed immediately. That money is out of my bank account, so I cannot spend it. Otherwise, I will find myself in a pickle. I've been there before, in my twenties. I'm sure everyone has. Not significant debt, but more debt than I should have been in then.

These coping mechanisms help me because it means that I don't have to be organised; I just have to do it once in a while. If I put it by, the bank does everything else. I suspect it's part of my autistic tendencies that I need to have some control. No one else is going to help me with finances and I cannot find myself in a position where I can't afford something or other. Even my pet rats have a debit card and bank account, and X amount goes in every month for them. When they're young, fine, you save a hundred or so a month, and then when they do get sick, you might blow five hundred pounds in four weeks. You can get rat insurance, but it's more expensive than saving up. Little things like that mean I'm never caught unawares.

I look at some of my friends who don't have these mechanisms. When I talk to them about it, they're like, 'I never thought of that.' But how do people deal with their money otherwise? If my money were all in one place, I would spend it and be in a massive heap of trouble. I am also bad at numbers: dyscalculia, although not officially diagnosed. I transpose numbers a lot, so spreadsheets are my friend.

If everything is in a bank account or a spreadsheet, I know I'm organised. I'm much more comfortable, and I have less anxiety. I hate that feeling of stress. If I can do something that prevents it from a long-term perspective, I will put it into place – so long as I remember.

THE PROFESSIONAL VIEW

In 2019, CLARE SEAL faced a personal debt of twenty-seven thousand pounds, with no assets or safety net to help clear it. She paid it off in two years and documented this on her anonymous @myfrugalyear Instagram account. Now a qualified financial coach and the author of three books on money, Clare was diagnosed with ADHD in 2022.

The first thing – and it's really difficult – is to accept that sometimes things won't be perfect, and sometimes I will mess things up. That helps to solve the paralysis around starting anything. I had this huge debt and had tried quite a few times to resolve it before, and the one difference in the time that I managed it was that when I messed up, I kept going, instead of going back to the drawing board. Sometimes, you have to persevere with the same thing that has worked a little or imperfectly and try to get better at it.

There are some brilliant innovations in FinTech, so use all the digital tools available, like budgeting apps. I find Snoop really good, and there's Emma, there's Money Dashboard, and they will tell you your account balances every morning. You don't have to have that psyching yourself up to check your bank balance moment, forgetting to do it or forgetting that XY or Z payment is going out. It's really useful to have that at your fingertips rather than going into a budgeting spreadsheet or going into several different bank accounts.

Find things that make it easier, like automating payments and putting everything you can on a direct debit or a standing order. That's another thing that you don't have to use that executive part of your brain for. Having an accountability partner or a way of holding yourself accountable is essential, especially if you're trying to save for long-term goals. When I was paying off my debt, I used a grid where I coloured in a square every time I paid off 1 per cent, which was visually helpful. Find a way to motivate yourself that works for you, and the second it stops working, find something else to replace it rather than letting your interest dwindle.

The combination of ADHD and the self-employed tax system is lethal, especially when you're talking about things like payments on account and the fact that, when my accountants do my tax return for me, it's just a random number that never bears any resemblance to what I've calculated, even if I've done it with all of the tax calculators. The combination of impulsive spending and having a boatload of money set aside for tax you're not supposed to touch is really dangerous. Having certain non-negotiable things is important because if I allow things to be fluid or open to interpretation, the whole structure completely falls apart. What might be a set structure that works for you? If it's treating savings the same way you treat your rent, then thinking, 'This has to be paid every month. This is just another bill,' can be helpful.

With Starling, you can create a bills pot, tick what you want to go out of there, then it will tell you how much it is, and you can set it to transfer that amount. Loads of these FinTech developments are really helpful for ADHD and embracing things that will make your life easier is a big thing. I know loads of people, including myself quite often, who feel they should be able to operate like everyone else does. Remember, these things have made life easier for neurotypical people, too; it's just that the impact for us is even more significant. Anything that you can automate, anything that someone else can do for you – grasp it with both hands. It may all make a big difference. Accepting those times when everything's ebbing and knowing that the tide will turn at some point is almost a mantra I hold myself to.

Cheatsheet: Your financial toolkit

You Need A Budget (YNAB): This is just brilliant if you have a regular salary. Hyperfocus on setting it up using the many YouTube videos; suddenly, you can oversee all your money.

Snoop, Emma, Money Dashboard, Monzo, Starling: Banking apps that let you create pots (and decorate everything nicely) to track your spending and savings.

Accountability partners: A friend or a coach – Clare uses her Instagram community to keep herself going.

Automate everything: Direct debits and standing orders are our best friends and keep money for bills out of sight and out of mind.

Have a separate bank account for business: If you can, pay yourself a set amount each month.

Check your phone subscriptions: Ensure you aren't paying for apps you don't use. If print subscriptions are your kryptonite, Readly is a great app that collects almost every magazine and newspaper in one app for £9.99 a month.

Find a way to motivate yourself: The second it stops working, find something else to replace it rather than letting your interest dwindle.

CHAPTER ELEVEN

Parenting with ADHD

I was always ambivalent about whether I wanted to be a mother. Practically, a fear of getting pregnant had been embedded into all of us at school. Parenting also seemed to be bloody hard, and I found life quite difficult enough when it was just me, but when I met my husband, I couldn't imagine anything better than having children with him. That ambivalence didn't magically disappear when we got married, not least because I was soon made redundant the following month for a third time. Having spent my twenties feeling untethered, I wanted security for my children. How could I get that if I wasn't secure?

For something I wasn't sure about, I really tried to have children. As it was, it didn't happen for us. We had some fertility tests, leading to two failed IVF cycles and a non-diagnosis of 'unexplained infertility'. I was a stark, broken mess. I started seeing a new therapist, and we did a lot of work around infertility, identity and shame. The following year, my husband and I looked into trying again, only for a new consultant to say it wouldn't work. We looked into adoption, but after the past few years, we were fried. A small voice told me I wasn't mentally well enough for the responsibility anyway. I know some people who have adopted, and they are definitely human, but they are also rocks. I did not feel like a rock.

When I started seeing a new therapist about ADHD, we didn't speak about kids or infertility until one day, I mentioned that it was probably better that I didn't have children because of my brain. My new therapist looked at me in a particular way and said gently and deliberately, 'ADHD does not mean you would be a bad parent. Lots of people with ADHD have children. Lots of them are wonderful parents.' I didn't know how much I needed to hear that. Slowly, I am becoming involved with the children in my life. Their parents gave me grace for this slowness, and I am grateful. Little traditions are taking seed. There are trips to the circus, walks with the dog, and the solidity of being there. I enjoy seeing glimpses of the people these children will become. Equally, as a non-parent, I am thrilled to have an excuse to hide away with the dog during the sonic chaos of teatime. Interviewing parents with ADHD has been weirdly healing, particularly about how their parenting compares to their upbringing or those of their parents. Thank you to everyone making things clearer and better for the next generation and those that came before.

DANIELLE, 44: When the pandemic hit, it was a perfect storm of events. Our second child was ten weeks old. Melbourne went in and out of lockdown for two years. My eldest started to have some really big emotions, and I just remember sitting there watching him and thinking, 'Fuck, I would love to do that. I'd love to be able to just lose my shit,' but I know that's not socially acceptable. That's when I realised I was trying to teach him skills I don't have. I had started to institute a quiet time when they weren't allowed to play with toys that talked. For two hours a day, I could be free of those annoying, jarring sounds that you're just supposed to suck up for hours on end when you're an adult. I remember thinking, 'I can't wait till they get old enough for me to hire a rage room, take all these toys there and smash the shit out of them.' Once I got the diagnosis, the parenting quickly got a lot better, and I got better because I was regulated, so that brought the temperature down.

FIONA, 53: I've got three children. Two have got university exams. One has just finished his Scottish exams. I am trying to claim back time for me, and I think that my cancer helped that because they have become much more independent. They do their own laundry when they come home. It's not so helpful with the chaos but then that's because of my ADHD; the house is carnage and I'm always tidying. We're very lucky in that there's a Scottish initiative where kids get free bus tickets so instead of rushing to pick my daughter up at the airport, or wherever she might be, I tell her to get the bus. Saying, 'No, you need to plan your time,' is a huge deal for me. She had a strop the other day when I told her I couldn't take her somewhere because I was going for a walk with a friend. That's the first time that I didn't drop everything. My daughter has ADHD, of course, and I have my suspicions my sons may have it, and it's really important that they put processes in place for helping themselves.

We need people to be accepting of others who are neurodiverse but there was some real merit in good old-fashioned traditional qualities in our formative years; ones that I didn't really have. I'm worried people might now go, 'You don't need to know that because you've got ADHD,' or, 'Oh, no, that will just confuse you.' We do form neural pathways; we just have to do something over and over again. Having taught English, learning by rote isn't always bad, and it's relevant to other elements of neurodiversity. I don't think education now allows time for practising. People don't know what they don't know until it's too late, and the education system isn't geared up for people with ADHD at the best of times. There are loads of apps now, but if you're learning how to track your finances, for example, you're probably learning that at home, and if your parents also have ADHD and haven't addressed it, that doesn't make life that easy for you. School could help by teaching revision timetabling and how to study. You learn but don't get taught to revise – or maybe that's just Scotland. I struggled. I started doing law at university, and I dropped out. Looking back, it was because I couldn't cope. There were so many cases to learn, and I didn't revise in time.

SEAN, 38: I wish I'd known more about ADHD when my son was a baby. He had terrible colic and was just really bad at breastfeeding. I fully get that breast is best, but we felt genuinely shamed by the nurses for resorting to bottles, and it's like this baby's starving. He's screaming twenty hours a day. Not that it would have changed how I felt, but it just would have been nice to know then that like, oh, by the way, you are probably finding this harder than most people because you have trouble regulating your emotions. There were plenty of instances where I did cry with him, but every time he cried, I was like, 'Oh my God, it's like this is happening to me.' It was amazing that that bond was so immediate, but it was difficult not to shut that out. I know people who would put noise-cancelling headphones on when the baby's upset, and I'm just like, 'What the fuck?' It wouldn't work because I can still see what's happening, and there's just no way of me shutting that out, whereas other people seem to be able to keep a lid on it.

Sleep deprivation doesn't help. I was dealing with really bad anxiety during that whole period. I started getting paranoid that I would get ill, the baby would get ill, my wife would leave me; these constant suspicions coming out of nowhere. I spoke to a therapist on Better Help, that app-based therapy thing, who asked, 'How much sleep are you getting?' I said, 'About three hours a night.' 'Okay, probably get some more sleep and see if that helps.' In three days, I was fine.

The medication helps with emotional regulation but doesn't magically fix it. It's not okay if you lose your temper, but you can forgive yourself more quickly. I know why that was hard, even though all the research says that shouting doesn't help and you shouldn't do it. Some people say you have kids because you want a little version of yourself. Well, guess what? They will mirror all the stuff you don't like about yourself as well as the stuff you do. Equally, when you make decisions for the child's mental health, you realise they're probably helping you as well: it's very easy for me to play *Zelda* for a bit, and then 'a bit' becomes an hour and a half. Now that we're trying absolutely no screen time, apart from a bit of CBeebies when he's getting ready for school, he's in a much better mood, and I think I am as well.

The weather has picked up in the last few weeks, so we're doing more stuff in the garden. He loves gardening, which is lovely because I always struggled with that. When I was a kid, my dad wanted me to be into gardening, and my granddad wanted me to be into fishing, which are both complete nightmare hobbies if you've got ADHD. I'm better now at enjoying more peaceful activities, although I'm still bad at getting myself to sit down and read a book.

Trying fishing again now would be interesting. As a child, I remember my granddad telling me off because I was running around and him explaining that the fish can sense the vibrations and they'll all bugger off.

EMILY, 48: In the first year after my daughter's dad and I split up, she was acting out, and I complained to a friend how awful I felt because this is what she was doing, and it's because I'm a single parent. My friend said, 'You've got to stop looking at everything this way. It has to do with the fact that three-year-olds are assholes. This isn't on you. This is just life.' There's something about hearing other people's stories, even if they don't have the answers, and knowing that there are other travellers with you on the road that is really rewarding. There's great power in parenting ourselves. One of the best things about getting to parent my daughter is that I get to do things the way I wish they had been done to me. With ADHD, I see that as an opportunity to ask myself what I wish I had heard.

When my daughter was in Reception, she came home one day in hysterical tears and said, 'Star called me a chicken nugget-foot-head.'

'Oh my God, that's awful,' I said. 'So, are you?'

'What?'

I said, 'Well, are you a chicken nugget-foot-head?'

'No.'

I said, 'Then why are you upset? Because Star said it, does it make it true? Are you upset that she said something mean to you? Just because someone tells you something doesn't make it true about yourself.'

That's one of the parenting things I think of a lot. When someone says, 'Everybody's a little ADHD,' it doesn't mean it's true. When people say ADHD is a superpower, it doesn't mean it's true. I get to decide what ADHD is for me, and sometimes I need to ask myself: Are you a chicken nugget-foot-head? If you hear someone say, 'All these women are just using this as an excuse, and how do people spend their entire lives not knowing they have this thing?', my answer is: because I spent my entire life thinking that I didn't fit in, that I was useless, and everyone else had a handle on things in a way that I didn't because I was shit, not because there was something wrong with me.

JAMES, 47: Childhood labels stay with you. I've always been really hot on that in my parenting. I will not label my child because I'm aware that if you say, 'Oh, you're sensitive,' they'll then believe they're a sensitive person, and that won't ever go away. You don't ever do things like that. ADHD mainly manifested for me when my daughter was very young because children are deeply tedious at that age. I mean that in the best possible way, but they are not conversationalists. Once the novelty of 'I made a thing, and it moves!' wears off, you're just like, 'I've watched eighteen episodes of Peppa Pig back to back, and I want to kill myself.' Things that some people find easy, like playing with a small child, I found intensely challenging. I have a very specific kryptonite zone, which is when something requires a sufficient focus that you can't do it while doing something else, but it's not interesting enough that I can commit my whole brain to it. I found that with my child when she was a toddler. I loved her to bits and loved spending time with her, but it was killing me to have to do infantile things like singing songs because it just wasn't interesting.

The workaround I found was, instead of reading to her from children's books, I read to her from adult books. I bought *A Little History of the World* by E. H. Gombrich, which covered everything from the prehistoric era to the American Civil War in a very palatable, digestible way. If you've ever seen *Three Men and a Baby*, there's a bit where Tom Selleck is reading to the baby from *Sports Illustrated* about a boxing match, and he was like, 'It doesn't matter what you say, it's the tone you use.' I read from the book very animatedly, and she loved it – obviously didn't understand a word of it – but I was learning stuff, so I wasn't bored, and she was spending time with me, so we found this middle ground. That persisted until she was about five, and then, once she became quite a good conversationalist, it all became a lot easier. She's eleven now and the most articulate person you'll ever meet. I've never spoken to her like she's a child because that would have bored me. I remember walking through the supermarket and some women laughing because I was explaining the American electoral college system to a six-year-old. I'm sure it all went over her head, but because I was engaged with it, she was interested in listening.

CLEMENTINE, 36: I didn't cope initially. I still have days where I don't cope in the same way that all parents have days they don't cope. Being a parent is multitasking, constantly choosing what's most important to do, and making sure you get that right every single day. It just completely blew my fuse. In some respects, I wasn't put on this earth to be a parent, even though I've always wanted to be a mum. I love being a mum, and my girls are my absolute world, but I sometimes feel bad that they've managed to end up with me because I find it difficult. One child asks me something; the other asks me something. From what I've read about neurotypical people – and I feel funny about that term – I don't hear two voices. It does something to me, and I want to explode; I can't cope, and they're not my children any more; they're noise. I don't know how to explain it because I know there's not a second I don't love them. It's not like they become objects that I don't love. But when they're making so much noise, my brain says, 'Turn that noise off.'

Having children is probably a big factor in how and when I got diagnosed because all my traits came out. I still struggle with the concept of 'done is enough' because I'm a perfectionist, and if I'm going to do something, it needs to be perfect, which is another reason parenting has broken me in a way because you can't be perfect. It is impossible to be a perfect parent. From spilling their orange juice to burning their jacket potato to buying the wrong colour pyjamas, you're not going to get it right because you're dealing with miniature tricky people. I've had to find coping strategies; otherwise, I would have had a breakdown. For noise, I use Loop earbuds. They don't mute my children – I don't *want* to mute my children – but they help my brain deal with the volume and the cacophony. I'll use them on the school run when my children are chatting really loudly. Without my Loops in, I'm constantly saying, 'I'm one metre away; you're talking to me like I'm several metres away. I'm right here,' while my youngest goes, 'WHAT?'

I don't like loud noise at all, never have. My parents divorced when I was very young, and I remember the screaming most. I would cry, not because I was scared – I was too young to factor in that Mummy and Daddy were fighting – it was the noise. My brain says, 'No, I don't like that. Stop it immediately.' Loops are amazing; and then mindfulness. I think I'll be trying to get better at it until the day I die, partly because I don't do it enough, or I find an excuse not to, or I lose my colouring book. Colouring is something I find very calming. I don't colour in because I particularly enjoy the artistic outcome; I do it because it's like a brain factory reset. It's an amazing way to regain focus when I'm feeling overwhelmed by too many thoughts flying around in my head.

ANDY, 52: I remember trying to explain to my mum that I thought I was different and something was wrong with me. My parents are both doctors. I wore my heart on my sleeve about the whole thing, and she said, 'No, no, you're fine. You're perfectly fine.' I can see she was thinking there was some stigma, and I guess she was trying to be reassuring by telling me everything was fine, but I knew it wasn't because I was struggling. I could have used a bit more support, even if it was just emotional, and that has definitely affected my parenting style. I'm trying to ensure that I don't make the mistakes my parents did with me, although, obviously, I'm going to make a whole bunch of new ones that I won't even know about for another ten years.

Destigmatising is a big, big part of that, understanding our little foibles and traits and being okay with them. There's a great line from the movie *Little Miss Sunshine* where they're about to get pulled over, and the dad says, 'Everybody, just pretend to be normal!' I realised I've spent my entire life with people telling me that. You do that for half a century, and it takes a toll. It grinds away your self-image, and it's stressful. It never works because it's not who you are.

The flip side of that with parenting is we still need to function in the world as it is. We might try to improve it while we're in it, but we've still got to get by, so it's trying to strike the right balance. You can't just withdraw from it completely. The key for me, rather than telling my kids this is what you should do or what you shouldn't, is helping them figure out who they are and then laying down track in front of whichever direction they go in to help them find the best version of themselves, rather than force them into being somebody else.

THE PROFESSIONAL VIEW

GRACE TIMOTHY is the author of Mum Face: The Memoir of a Woman Who Gained a Baby and Lost Her Sh*t and the host of the podcast Is It My ADHD? She was diagnosed at age thirty-seven when her daughter was eight.

Before I'd even heard of ADHD, I would have assumed any issues were because parenting is a lot, and I know I share that with all of my friends to varying degrees. Now, when I drill down into what I found challenging, it's all related to overwhelm, particularly sound. It does seem to be that intersection of ADHD pounding away at how you deal with universal challenges; so sleep deprivation, for example, which for us was two years, in retrospect, had a huge impact on my ADHD in terms of executive function. You could argue that that was fairly normal, but I wrote an entire book about it, and when I look back, oh my gosh, hello, it was ADHD all along.

The dialogue around parenting was only just starting to shift when I had my daughter in 2012. There was still this sense as a parent that you are eternally grateful, which we all are. You embrace every moment! When they wake you up at three o'clock, it might be the last time they ever do that, so hold them close! There was always this sense of impending doom that this would be over in a flash, you'll never get it back, and you'll grieve for the rest of your life, so that massively plays into your guilt and shame around finding things difficult.

When my book was commissioned, a few publishers said it wasn't for them because I was writing about those feelings. One said she had an absolutely amazing maternity leave; her work had been really supportive, and she loved her daughter, so it didn't resonate with her. The idea that she loved her child so didn't relate to the difficult stuff made me go, 'Okay, I'm going to throw up now.' The book came out as we saw a general shift in the parenting conversation through Instagram, but I think we also know that, with ADHD, shame is something that you've carried with you from the minute you first open your mouth and say something weird. It played into parts of me that I acknowledged were there but didn't understand.

Through having had many, many conversations with different people with ADHD, I would suggest we do experience these things more acutely. Emotional regulation is more of a challenge. That's one of the reasons I found that aspect of parenting so difficult: I was grateful and deeply in love. The shame wasn't around wanting this child to go away, be different, shut up, or any of those things. It was wanting me to be able to handle it. At ten, my daughter is very aware of ADHD and autism because their generation just is, so I can be honest with her and say when I'm struggling. There are times when she finds that understandably frustrating, and others when it almost redresses the balance between us. She can see that we're both in the same boat, which has been quite helpful, and I can be empathetic if she's having a meltdown as I can see it more in terms of my own experience rather than thinking, 'Christ, you're just not complying, and you're being difficult on purpose.' It's about an un-codependent version of communicating with your child – I wouldn't share feeling suicidal with her, for example – and I apologise to her where it's relevant. She might remember my shouting at her about something because that's often what we hold on to as children, particularly if you are close to your parents and trust them. It's important to be able to say, 'I'm sorry. I think this is why that happened, but it's nothing to do with you, and I'm working on it.' If our children end up having relationships with people who have ADHD or have it themselves, that self-compassion is a crucial modelling tool that they need to see in action.

The main challenge as a parent for me is the sensory issue. My mum suffered from anxiety and depression, so we shared a slightly codependent set of tools. I knew about breathing and taking time out. I read a lot of parenting books, and I identified more closely with gentle parenting, which I riffed on by adding lots of boundaries, which perhaps you don't have as gentle parents, but also understanding that every awful moment that that child experiences is an opportunity for you to show your support and love for them and teach them that these things are normal. A lot of that teaching is that, for you to be compassionate, kind and empathetic, you need to not pour from an empty cup and to take time away and be your own person. Outwardly, that toolkit helped, and I was making good decisions, but internally, it didn't because I was ashamed that I was still relying on those things. I shouted at my daughter when I didn't want to shout at her. I could never quite be the person I knew I needed to be because another force was at play. I thought that was tiredness, but everyone's always tired, everyone in the whole world. It was this extra layer where I found the sound very difficult and triggering. When would you ever say that? I felt awful. I remember telling my husband that I couldn't take the screaming. I could say that in that very safe space in that safe relationship, but sound as a trigger was something I associated with the extremes of neurodivergence, and things where you can't cope in a normal society – there was so much stigma attached. Without someone saying, 'You have ADHD, you struggle with sound,' I would never have known that was the issue.

I'd found the first year of parenting the happiest and most calm and relaxed I'd ever been – my husband's view may differ. While getting up in the night was awful – it undid me in so many ways, and I couldn't function outside of my role as a mother – I found the baby dynamic of 'I'm going to shit when I want to shit, I'm going to scream when I want to scream' really straightforward. What got harder was when my daughter became a person with her own agency, and the outside world needed me in different ways. Even things like politics and engaging in the world were incredibly challenging and made me a far less patient parent. I could no longer recalibrate when there were tantrums. It's not like if a friend freaks out and you can say, 'Okay, we need some time apart.' This child is dependent on you, and you are so aware of that and want to do the very best you can for this person that you love.

The only reason it wasn't the straw that broke the camel's back was that my husband is very calm and grounding, and an excellent parent. I had a strong support network, so it couldn't get to a really dark place, but I acknowledge that it could have done. I did get therapy and there were a few moments where I admitted that I wasn't very happy. Nothing to do with how things were going as a parent or anything like that, just a core sense, which we know is something that comes and goes with ADHD. No one identified ADHD as being a player, it was all, 'You're tired.' I remember sex life coming up a lot and being like, 'Are you fucking joking? I've just had a baby.'

It almost needs to become that you prioritise anything that is required in a healthy way. Sleep has to be a priority. I cannot do nights out any more. Maybe I'll get back to that at some point, but now I just can't. Drinking doesn't suit me because I know that my patience will be at an all-time low. Watch out for that lack of dopamine if you're doing something mundane or at the three o'clock slump. I struggled with those fluctuating energy levels which affect us all – as a parent that's really tricky and you just have to pull yourself through. I remember sitting down to play Lego and falling asleep while I was doing it. It's not the right kind of stimulation, so you have an energy crash. On the flip side, someone with ADHD can be really good fun from a child's perspective, as long as you're not so dysregulated that you're unpredictable and frightening. I like that we have a laugh together; we giggle a lot and do all that stuff, which I'm sure happens outside ADHD, but these can make it a strength in parenting as much as it is an issue.

Cheatsheet: How to be an adult when you just want to explode

- Tag team your co-parent, family and friends so you can tap out
- Play to your strengths

- Prioritise your sleep
- Practising mindfulness helps give you that split second before going off on one
- Limit your alcohol consumption
- Communicate clearly so your child knows it isn't something that they have done (even if it totally is)

Telling your kid to take a breath, you're going to be okay, do you need a moment – those are my main tools. But also, sometimes they just need to hear, 'That's tough, I'm sorry to hear that,' from a parent. They don't need anything else.

– EMILY, 48

CHAPTER TWELVE

Hormones

For ages, this chapter was tumbleweed – not about people's experiences, but solutions. As the growing news around menopause shows, we are finally at a time of at least *some* coverage around subjects that only affect cis women, trans men and some non-binary people. We may be more than half the population, yet not the everyman. However, this burst hasn't yet coincided with significant research on hormones, let alone the impact of menstruation, pregnancy, childbirth and perimenopause on the brain, and still less when you factor in ADHD. My takeaway from three years of research about ADHD and hormones can best be summed up by the shrug emoji.

It's that overlap of not knowing much about ADHD, menopause coming into public awareness and the lack of training for GPs in something so fundamental. As has been the case for centuries, we're supposed to suck it up. With women now a force in the workplace, there is an economic reason for looking at menopause more closely (or at all). Only recently have women reached a point where they are considered objectively powerful enough to consider – and even then, only some women. Research funding into menopause remains pitiful. Research on hormones and ADHD is pretty much non-existent. It piles injustice on top of injustice, and it makes me so wildly cross. We're coming to terms with spending our lives undiagnosed, winging it somehow, and then the bloody menopause turns up the dial still further. Are you kidding me? I've only just got through IVF!

In my pre-menstrual weeks, I've felt like I am swimming through clouds more than usual, even with medication. In perimenopause, it feels like my medication doesn't hit the spot the week before and during my period. Hormones are an absolutely massive field of work, and when I'm not so livid about it, it's pretty exciting. I mean, I'd rather the work had already been done so we could benefit from it, but it still feels quite positive and uplifting to be a part of something that will hopefully help future generations. Of course, often it isn't exciting at all, and I need either to go to bed at teatime or to inhale a supermarket aisle of its most shelf-stable foods while weeping into the void and scrolling the internet in search of the perfect slogan baseball cap.

Being aware of my cycle at all is a concept I've only encountered in the past decade. I was on the pill for much of my twenties, and the rest of the time, the sheer existence of my period was a hazy concept until it would appear and take me entirely by surprise, despite happening every month since I was twelve. When I was trying to conceive, cycle-tracking apps had become a thing. I'd never tracked anything before – I lost paper and, pre-Google Docs, never owned a spreadsheet program – but apps made it easier, even if I usually drifted off and forgot to note when my period had ended. The monthly torture of the 'two-week wait' to see if I'd got pregnant meant that I tried to become even less aware of what was happening because it was too painful to have yet another reminder that I Had Failed At Being A Human Adult Woman. Now, I'm mostly aware of my period's imminent arrival by my desire to eat entire boxes of cereal before falling asleep.

When I think of how much information we were given at school about our periods, the lack of anything similar around menopause is sad, if not surprising given how little people are educated on fertility, let alone its tapering off. For many people, everything will be fine (I adore Amy Schumer's 'Last Fuckable Day' sketch, with Tina Fey, Julia Louis-Dreyfus and Patricia Arquette celebrating the descent into grandmotherly roles after years of being 'TV hot'). Still, for many others, especially those with untreated ADHD, it can be a nightmare, and you don't know why. While reading Heather Corinna's excellent book, *What Fresh Hell Is This?*, I was gobsmacked to learn that British GPs get two hours of training on menopause, something that 51 per cent of their patients will encounter. The cherry on top is that this training is optional – chef's kiss. In 2021, the campaigner Diane Danzebrink found through a freedom of information request that almost half of Britain's thirty-three medical schools did not have a mandatory teaching segment on menopause, with many saying they expected their students to be trained while on GP placement. She also found, as have I, that antidepressants, rather than hormone replacement therapy, are commonly suggested as the first line of treatment. Grimly, female suicide rates in Britain are highest for women aged forty-five to fifty-four: the average perimenopause and early post-menopausal years.

I have done bloodwork, all of which has returned saying my hormone levels are fine, but my fertility tests told me the same thing. One of my grandmothers completed menopause at forty-four – an outlier as far as I know, but enough for me to think that could be why I have symptoms, which I have been sporadically tracking since I was thirty-eight. If and when they worsen, I will ask my GP for HRT, but I don't think I have the heart to go through yet another edition of 'Guess what I think is wrong with me this time!'

What is clear is that my periods are becoming increasingly like emotional horror films. I'd never heard of PMDD [premenstrual dysphoric disorder, a severe form of premenstrual syndrome, also known as PMS or PMT, which are the physical and mental symptoms in the days before a period] before my therapist, who is an ADHD specialist, said, 'Ah, you have this, don't you?' I replied, 'No, I'm just a horrible person who's bad around my period, but it's my fault, not anything else.' I've seen women in every ADHD community anecdotally report that their symptoms worsen during PMS and PMDD and that their medications have less effect on them during that time. I was medicated when I got done for speeding. The pills aren't bombproof. I was merrily doing ninety miles an hour down a motorway and was rightly stopped by the police. I am now significantly more wary of when I drive and how I feel when doing so, and I maintain a very close relationship with the cruise control button.

'There's a good biological, theoretical framework for what so many women are telling us: that their medication is not working in the same way depending on where in their menstrual cycle they are, and that their ADHD symptoms are fluctuating along with their hormones,' says the psychiatrist and ADHD researcher Lotta Borg Skoglund, author of *ADHD Girls to Women: Getting on the Radar*. 'It's beginning to be acknowledged in scientific literature, but it has been a huge knowledge gap – and really, neither scientists nor healthcare professionals have been interested.' If you have a cool million or so burning a hole in your pocket, why not consider funding research into hormones and ADHD?

HANNAH, 50: Looking back, my ADHD exploded as a teenager. I can see a huge correlation between going through puberty and risk-taking. I was always looking for a dopamine hit and in the wrong places, you know, smoking and drinking, boys. It was almost like I couldn't stop myself from doing stuff even though I knew it wasn't right. I'd be in the moment and just had to do it because it was exciting and thrilling. There was a lot of guilt that came out of making these decisions. A lot of shame that I carried around with me for a long time. I felt like I was in a vicious cycle; I kept making the same mistakes. It wasn't until I was in my mid-thirties and first saw a therapist that I was able to let some of the guilt and shame go.

Perimenopause became very apparent when I took a course, had to write essays, and couldn't string any thoughts together. It was like someone had vacuumed out my brain. Before I was diagnosed with ADHD at forty-eight, I'd noticed my brain fog would get really bad in the week leading up to my period. As I got more into my perimenopause, the brain fog would last for two weeks. Then it got to the point where it was three weeks, and I had a week of feeling like a normal human being. That's when I started looking into ADHD and menopause, and it made sense. ADHD medication and HRT have helped, but it's not a magic pill; it doesn't get rid of it completely.

MICHELLE, 41: I was diagnosed with PMDD about five years ago, before ADHD. I think I was probably incorrectly diagnosed. I say incorrectly: I took it to the doctor because I thought this was the only thing it could be. Ten days before my period, I became this person. What else could it be? People don't talk about ADHD, so why would I have even considered that being a possibility?

The hormonal challenges do not get better now I'm being treated for ADHD, sadly. Ten days before my period, I can't concentrate. My medication basically doesn't work, so I bite my tongue in meetings. I find myself highly emotional about having to mask because, obviously, no dopamine, can't do anything.

I've tried many variants of my medication up to 70mg Elvanse, and all that did was keep me up for twenty-four hours, so I ended up on 70mg of Elvanse and then taking melatonin to wake up and go to sleep. But while that helped make me a bit more awake (with PMS, you want to sleep when you're exhausted and more so when you're not interested in stuff), nothing has helped with the anger. No one sees I'm angry, but I am spitting feathers and swearing at them inside. My doctor put me on something called Clonidine to reduce the anxiety, and if I don't take it, it's like Attila the Hun is inside my head.

Those are symptoms that I would have classed as PMDD, but there's so much overlap between that and untreated ADHD it's really difficult to tell where one starts and the other ends. I just do the thing. If it works, then yay. And if it doesn't, I will stay in my house for a week. It's not only the ten days that I lose. I still get stuff done, but I'll have to sit on my laptop for eighteen hours to do it and I'll be exhausted. If we could get my hormones to do whatever they're supposed to do, it would be so much more helpful for me and my job because I can't explain how difficult it is to function.

CLEMENTINE, 36: Having children turned my ADHD from a small signpost to a giant flashing neon sign. It turned everything upside down. My husband says to me now, 'It's so weird, you didn't seem to have ADHD before we had children.' And I say the bottom line is I had to have done because you don't just *get* it. You don't brush against someone and pick it up. I picked a few scenarios and asked, 'Do you remember what I did? Remember when I did that? That was ADHD.' The point is I didn't have triggering factors around me constantly pushing me. Before my beautiful children were born, I'd created a world I could live in alongside my ADHD and where I could function.

BETHAN, 42: I have a lot of what I call 'non-drive days', where I'm not safe in a car. It's not something I've historically had a problem with. It's something that's getting worse as I get older. I've started tracking it on a sheet, putting an X for different symptoms on different days. It's usually around day fourteen and maybe during the first few days of my period, but sometimes, I don't know until I'm in the car, and then I need to stop and leave it wherever it is.

Nothing bad has ever happened; it's more clumsiness. I once got stuck on the same two roundabouts in Newport while trying to get a Christmas tree. I've been on these roundabouts my entire driving life, and I couldn't work out how to get in the right lane. I was on the roundabout for, I shit you not, forty-five minutes. When I ended up at the garden centre, I was on the phone with my boyfriend, crying, and he was like, 'Just come home,' but I was going, 'I want a *real* tree!' When I went home, I had forgotten the tree. But then I drove back the next day, and it was a 'drive day', and it was fine.

There are other times when I feel overwhelmed, and I've been trying to get out of a parking space and banged against the pillars, and I've just been like, 'Fuck, I've got to get out of the car.' It affects my spatial awareness, I think. My depth perception has never been amazing anyway, and I also find it difficult to look at stripes, which people think is hilarious. If you look down the escalator, sometimes the treads look normal. Then, other times, I can't look at them properly. On that day, when I couldn't get out of the car park, I bumped the car again into the neighbour's car. I just reversed into it for no reason at all. Things are happening too fast, and you can't slow them down or do your normal mirror, signal, manoeuvre. It's like the world is happening to you instead of the other way around.

ANNABELLE, 51: Things kicked off after I had my kids. When I had my daughter, I thought it was loneliness that I was feeling. Then I'd see all the other mums, and they'd have everything regimented, whereas every time I tried to get the pram out of the car, it would take an age. I guess it was the self-doubt of, 'Why aren't I as practical as everybody else?' Socially, I've never really had problems. That's one of the great benefits of having ADHD; it's that chameleon thing where we can mask and fit in. But after my daughter, and my son's birth eighteen months later, I couldn't cope. I hated myself because I saw everybody else managing and didn't know what was wrong with me.

In the third lockdown, I hit the menopause. Oh. My. God. I was suicidal for the first time. I'd heard menopause was bad, but this was beyond. I was like, 'Get me on HRT,' and because I've got chronic cirrhosis, they had to do loads of checks. I was working in mental health and addiction, and it was during ADHD training that I heard about inattentive ADHD, and I thought, 'Hang on a second' – honestly, the hairs on the back of my neck stood up – 'that's me.' The more research I did, going down these rabbit holes – 'that's me'. I'd always presumed it was the naughty boys sitting on the naughty step, but for girls, it goes inwards, and during puberty and menopause, it shows up exponentially. I did go on HRT, which, my God, helps so much with the brain fog. I'm still completely ADHD in everything I do, but physically, I don't feel so stressed or tired.

FIONA, 53: I was diagnosed with ADHD at the end of April. They were very thorough, despite my GP being cynical. I've got the same type as my daughter. I had enforced menopause because my cancer was oestrogen-based, and my psychiatrist said that it is really common now for women who are menopausal to discover that they have ADHD.

I had an appointment with my GP a couple of days ago, and she is trying her damnedest to be supportive, but you can tell she is still so cynical. Sadly, there are predatory people out there, which enforces the cynicism. But weirdly, I spoke to the breast cancer nurse just after my ADHD diagnosis, and they use a drug, Clonidine, for enforced menopause, which is also used for ADHD. You'd have thought they might have worked that one out themselves, wouldn't you? My GP is pleading dumb even though the breast cancer nurse says it's very clearly on the NHS website as the first port of call. It's extraordinary that it can be used for both, but there might be other reasons I couldn't take it, and I've obviously got to respect that.

THE PROFESSIONAL VIEW

DR LOUISE NEWSON is a GP and menopause specialist and the founder of the Menopause Charity. She is a member of the Government Menopause Taskforce, and her many works include two bestselling books, the Balance app and website, and the Dr Louise Newson podcast.

For many years, it's all about periods and fertility when it comes to hormones. The three sex hormones – oestrogen, progesterone and testosterone – get into our bloodstream, but more importantly, they go into our brain and work as neurotransmitters. They can affect how other parts of our brain work and how other chemicals and neurotransmitters work in our brain. We don't know much about it because no one's done any studies. No one really cares about female hormones and their effect on their brain! I've got three daughters, so I know the power of hormones in female brains in adolescence, but because it's short-lived, no one does much about it. Even in pregnancy, we are warned that we could have 'baby blues' or feel a bit low. No one does anything about it because hormones typically go back to a stable level, but for many women, they don't.

What we see a lot in perimenopause is that traits from when the patient was younger can become exaggerated, so symptoms of ADHD can manifest again. It is the same as symptoms of anxiety, low mood, addictions or eating disorders – they can all come back because our brain is in this flux. We don't know whether it's the level of hormones or the changing levels. My guess is it's more the latter. Our brains like homeostasis; they like things to be in equilibrium, and when they're not, well, we all know when we're hangry.

Myth-busting: What is the link between oestrogen and dopamine?

All these transmitters, oestrogen and testosterone and dopamine, work together, so there's this constant bias feedback. Our reward system is probably more testosterone- than oestrogen-driven. Still, we've got receptors for oestrogen and testosterone in our brain's reward centre, which is often also triggered by dopamine.

We're writing up a paper with a neuroscientist in Michigan who's done a lot of work looking at the role of dopamine and testosterone in mice – not saying that women are mice – and the behaviours are very similar to people who are perimenopausal or menopausal. The other thing is, I think more women are testosterone-deficient than oestrogen-deficient, so there will be a lot of women who will not be perimenopausal. Still, their testosterone level will be low enough that it's having a detrimental effect on the way their brain works. That's something we've just not researched because everyone says testosterone's for libido, but it does make quite a difference elsewhere.

What's driving the conversation around ADHD and PMDD?

PMDD is related to hormones and is a whole spectrum as well. Just before the period, oestrogen is at its lowest, and progesterone is also low. So, some women respond well to oestrogen, some respond really well just to progesterone, and some need testosterone, too. It shows that we are all different in how our hormones interact with each other.

We also know that hormones, especially pro-gesterone, work better if people are not stressed and eat a really good diet. I wonder about some of the processing of food and how that can affect how our hormones bind to our receptors – there's so much we don't know. We all know that when we're feeling a bit shit and our hormone levels are low, we won't eat or exercise as well. It's all connected, but we've looked at things in isolation for far too long: 'If this woman exercises with PMDD, she'll feel better.' Yeah, but try getting her off the sofa when she feels dreadful. Please don't make her feel worse because she's not exercising. If you give back the hormones that have dropped, just as a small dose, that will make her feel better, so she'll exercise more, and everything will fall into place. That's what's important.

If menopause blood tests come back negative, what can people do to see if they are in perimenopause?

The blood tests are not reliable. Hormone levels can change, so it's looking at what blood tests are being done and what time they're done. Monitoring symptoms is essential. If symptoms vary throughout the menstrual cycle in people still having periods, it's likely related to hormones. That's useful for us as specialists to look at how it changes symptoms. If your hormone blood tests are normal, it's still worth talking to somebody.

Education is critical because knowledge is power. When we say HRT, it sounds a bit harsh because that's hormone replacement therapy. We're not replacing hormones; we're topping them up. It's more like hormone support treatment; all we do is give back what's missing, which can make a huge difference.

LOTTA BORG SKOGLUND is an associate professor in psychiatry at the Department of Women's and Children's Health at Uppsala University. Her scientific research targets the intersection of ADHD and comorbid conditions, gender discrepancies and hormonal factors. She is the author of ADHD Girls to Women: Getting on the Radar.

The first thing we have to establish is that ADHD is the same condition, it's the same disorder, it's the same impairment in men and women, but, on a group level, females tend to display ADHD symptoms differently. We think that has to do with both biology and social expectations.

On a group level – and it's really important to stress that because there are a lot of girls who will not feel that they could see themselves in that description, and a lot of boys who would typically feel much more at home in the description of how girls feel and display their symptoms – it seems like girls tend to mature and to realise what people expect from them at an earlier age. That means girls can adapt their behaviour, mask and find strategies for their difficulties earlier. The people around them can then wrongly think that they don't have any impairment or that they're not struggling, but they are.

Then puberty hits, and hormones are all over the place. On a group level, it seems like females display a more externalising profile; the paradox is that we miss them again because then we tend to look at their difficulties from a social or psychosocial view. We'd say that they are attention-seeking, outgoing or extrovert, or even risk-taking or sexually advanced. And then also, of course, they present with comorbidities like anxiety and depression, where they have tried to find ways to cope with their difficulties. Their strategies have either gone bad or become destructive and really dangerous, such as self-harm or eating disorders. Females do have hyperactivity and impulsivity but might display this in a slightly different way. Hyperactivity can be emotions or feelings all over the place; impulsivity might be more of the verbal type than the classic behavioural impulsivity we're used to looking for in boys.

Four to ten years before menopause, you enter perimenopause, and your hormones fluctuate similarly to puberty. It's fluctuating and then fluctuating. Many women describe increased emotional instability, brain fog and decreased cognitive functioning to an extent that they fear that they are developing dementia. Problems associated with ADHD can be enhanced, like sleeping problems and being more sensitive to stimuli from your own body, so increased sensitivity to pain and being much more sensitive to external stimuli like heat and cold, so hot flashes. It's basically an intense version of ADHD symptoms overlapping with common symptoms of menopause.

We know that dopamine, an essential neurotransmitter dysregulated in ADHD, is intimately associated with oestrogen levels. In periods where we have higher oestrogen levels, like before ovulation, in pregnancy, and in other conditions, you have a certain defence. You are vulnerable when oestrogen levels are low or fluctuating. Oestrogen affects your body temperature, cognitive functions and emotional regulation abilities, so during this perimenopausal and menopausal phase, females are especially vulnerable to also having their ADHD symptoms get worse. We think there might be some kind of ratio there with oestrogen–testosterone levels in females, which might also affect ADHD symptoms, but we are far from knowing exactly how that plays out.

The message is that there is perhaps not a silver bullet but rather a need to get back down to the essentials of life; the backbone of what is fundamental for mental health for everyone but essential when you have ADHD, especially if you are in a hormonal fluctuation or a vulnerable period of your cycle.

Make sure you tend to those routines even more carefully; all the basic things of diet, sleep, stress and physical activity. Avoid alcohol and be especially attentive to your emotions and your relationships. List the things you know can get worse and try to predict them: I see that so many females realise this, but they realise it three days afterwards. I call it 'broken record syndrome'. It's not helpful for someone to tell you that, but it would be helpful if you could send a message to yourself into the future and say, 'Okay, in two weeks, this is probably going to happen. What should I do? Well, I should tend to myself and be extra careful to keep my everyday routines. I have to nurse myself like an infant during this period.'

There's what you can do yourself and then what you can discuss with your healthcare professional. For menopause, there might be hormone replacement therapy, and for reproductive age and during the menstrual cycle, hormonal contraceptives can flatten out your hormonal fluctuations so that you don't get as affected as you would if they were fluctuating as normal.

DR ELLIE DOMMETT: One area spanning social inequalities which our lab will look into is women with ADHD and menopause. As I don't have ADHD, I wasn't aware of it, but I came across somebody who's neurodivergent and menopausal, and the HRT drought caused chaos in everything in her life. She couldn't keep up with anything because she'd lost her HRT and struggled to work out new ADHD meds. I've found some menopause experts at the university, and we're thinking of starting the process by asking menopausal women with ADHD what is the biggest challenge. Women's health is always less financed and has less awareness. There seems to be some weird mentality that we can give birth, so we should be able to survive anything. Women just get on with it. We know 15 to 20 per cent of the population have ADHD, and by adulthood, it's pretty equal on gender, so you could be talking 7 to 10 per cent of women who have ADHD and will all at some point go through menopause. There's a period where there are probably some difficulties at home, but that's also a workforce that is suddenly less productive and you're not necessarily putting in ways to allow them to maintain productivity. We want to look at that in the future, and again, I wonder if exercise will feed into that. I'm not familiar enough with how exercise and menopause go together, let alone throwing in ADHD. There's just so much that we don't know. You can't look at everything, so you've got to look at where the biggest gaps are: and for me that is exercise and women. If you think about people who have managed their adult ADHD with exercise, following a careful diet, or other tactics, everything falls apart when they lose their motivation. I have a friend who is unsure if she has depression or if it's perimenopause – she's not feeling quite right. We agree that I invite her whenever I run on a Monday. She's there dressed and ready to run every week, but she won't do it by herself.

Cheatsheet: ADHD and perimenopause

- Menopause marks a year to the day since your last period. Perimenopause is the transitional period involving symptoms for up to a decade before then. Fun!

- If you are on medication for ADHD but still experiencing significant brain fog, this may be a symptom of perimenopause. It is **highly unlikely** that you are experiencing early onset Alzheimer's, however much it may feel like it.

- Exercise, a decent diet and plenty of sleep are crucial. Keep a stock of easy, low- or no-prep meals and snacks (beans on toast; yoghurt, nuts, seeds, freezer fruit; apples, etc.). Leave your phone in another room to charge overnight. Read something undemanding and familiar before sleep. Choose an exercise that makes you happy and that you can slot in without thinking too hard about it. Walking, outdoor sessions, dancing, boxing, GoodGym, horse riding, personal training, Pilates, cycling, YouTube yoga – whatever floats your boat and feels fun.

- Track your symptoms. Dr Newson's free Balance app has a helpful tracker that you can set to those you experience regularly. Even if you don't remember to do it often, this will build up into a record both for medical professionals and to remind yourself that you aren't making this up.

- Even if you are unlikely to experience menopause, it will affect you. Educating yourself on symptoms is helpful so that you can support partners, friends, colleagues and random people sobbing on the Tube.

- *What Fresh Hell Is This?: Perimenopause, Menopause, Other Indignities, and You* by Heather Corinna is an inclusive, reassuring and very funny guide, perfect for the neurodivergent reader.

CHAPTER THIRTEEN

Self-medicating

In and of itself, what I use to self-medicate is not the problem. The problem is why.

I used to binge eat sweet food in zombie trances, and whenever I stopped for a while and lost some weight, I would get very upset. The extra weight offered me protection and comfort in a way I couldn't provide myself – I knew I could never lose enough to become what society expected a very tall woman to look like. When I started going to recovery meetings, it surprised me that hardly anyone talked about the substance, but rather, the feelings that led to them using it as an escape or a tool for numbing. A therapist once pointed out that I am terrible at sitting in discomfort, which is absolutely true. Boredom is other people's kryptonite; emotional discomfort is mine. Unease? No thank you! Please hand me the nearest treat.

My list of things I used to escape difficult feelings was longer than alcohol and food. It included doomscrolling Twitter, shopping, eBay saved searches, browsing the internet, MacGuffins (looking for 'the perfect' thing that actually doesn't exist), vaping, smoking, gardening, procrastination, basic chores, coffee, fads, lifestyles, book series and TV shows. Spending occasionally overlapped with a new interest – the Curly Girl hair method, eco cleaning, ethically made gym wear, skincare regimes – and then I'd get an extended dopamine hit from forking out money on things I'd intensely researched beforehand.

Sugar, cigarettes and alcohol were my main juggling act. When I was ten, I won a bottle of sherry at the village fete tombola and drank it with a school friend. God, it was revolting – if we tried more, maybe that would help. It did not help. Alcoholic drinks were, by and large, disgusting, but my desire to be like others and to shut my brain off was stronger. Cigarettes, too, I determined to master, pinching Silk Cut from my dad's sock drawer and going for long and entirely uncharacteristic walks around a field. Eventually, they became my props to punctuate boring days, conversations, small talk, anything remotely anxious-making and my act as a convincing human being.

After the nineties, when 'chocoholic' became a badge of honour, my most acceptable prop and one I didn't realise was treating my underlying ADHD symptoms, was coffee. (My ADHD pin-up, Dr Ned Hallowell, can't take meds, so he uses coffee instead.) My true love is tall, dark and at least 220 milligrams of caffeine. At youth theatre, I shrieked, 'Black coffee!' in a performance of Kander and Ebb's *Coffee in a Cardboard Cup*, and the sheer drama stuck with me. The only time I've weaned myself off sugar was when I stopped having three in my coffee (black, of course; the texture of most milk in coffee is revolting), simply because I was drinking so much of it and had no wish to know how much sugar I was spooning into each mug.

I drank coffee to calm down, focus, treat myself and make things more exciting. At an otherwise disappointing job, our office coffee machine was upgraded to rocket-ship status, and I was soon pounding the buttons to compensate. The coffees were never big enough, and rather than just adding more hot water, I lined up doubles. By the time I was drinking nine double-shot black Americanos a day, dignity had forced me to rethink my intake as I became very aware that coffee is a diuretic. Coffee also gave me my first brush with the idea of ADHD. I rocked up to my post-IVF therapy sessions clutching a bucket of black Americano as emotional support. 'You know, drinking a lot of coffee can be a sign of ADHD,' the therapist said. 'Huh!' I said, in the universal language of 'How interesting for someone who isn't me', and taking another huge swig. The coffee made so much sense. Unfortunately, the idea of coffee as a treat that helps me function is so ingrained that I've not yet cut the ties. Most pages of this book were written under the supervision of flat whites (the only good use of milk in coffee) and black Americanos. Even though I'm medicated, I don't need the caffeine and I can make coffee at home, I cannot let go of that association. Ordering decaf doesn't give me the same hit; it just makes me think I might as well pay for water – progress, not perfection. At least it's not alcohol.

I stopped smoking after the ban came in – although, if I got drunk, I became that annoying person creeping after your Marlboro Lights – but giving up alcohol was something I circled in confusion for years. I loved drinking, until the joy became joy and consequences, then primarily consequences. I never missed work because of a hangover. I certainly never drank in the morning. I never drank supermarket anything except cava, and I wasn't a middle-aged man with a red nose drinking super-strength cans on a park bench. I did not recognise the social image of being an alcoholic and thought if I tried harder, I'd regain control. Everyone else was doing something that I wasn't, and I just needed to try harder to be able to drink like them. Nothing too bad happened, but nothing to make me feel good. The final straw was when I used the death of my friend, Andrea, as an excuse to drink quite extensively. Every glass I had felt like a balloon with some of the air missing. The following day, I googled recovery meetings and was agog to sit in a room surrounded by people who could have walked out of my haunts, not off the park bench.

I assumed that once I stopped drinking, I would achieve my ultimate goal of becoming Deliciously Ella. I mean that quite sincerely. I think Ella Mills is fantastic and balanced, and I long to have the patience to treat myself that well and that thoughtfully. But giving up alcohol didn't get rid of the underlying reasons why I drank beyond simply being at a party; instead, it shone a hideous light on them. I dropped out of events because of panic attacks over what people might say. It took a long time for me to realise that much as I enjoyed getting pissed with people, I was also doing it as a social lubricant and that I found large gatherings quite difficult and preferred small groups with no small talk. I found dinners with loud conversations impossible to follow when sober, so I would simply zone out. I'm trying earplugs now to see if that will help make things a bit less 'everything everywhere all at once', as the Daniels' Oscar-winning film so beautifully puts it.

I initially replaced alcohol with black coffee and Ben & Jerry's ice cream, on the proviso that this was surely better than getting hammered and once again becoming a gigantic liability rampaging the streets of London. But I found food incredibly triggering. When I started secondary school, I'd started pinching packets of chocolate bars from my mum's carefully budgeted cupboards, eating the lot in a trance while sitting on my bedroom windowsill. The blissful feeling of absence never lasted long enough and was curbed by the knowledge that I would soon have some explaining to do about the missing chocolate. I tried making myself sick once after one of these binges, but I hated the feeling, the taste, and the idea that I would ruin my teeth even more than I already had the time I fell off my bike and landed on my face. I wanted to forget about the food once I'd eaten it, not see it again, and certainly not in a way that would be obvious to others.

The idea of people being aware of anything I did in secret was a nightmare on a level with being 'found out' as defective. Secrecy was paramount to my sense of safety. I've never had the urge to take my bra off at the end of the day (why are people wearing such uncomfortable bras!), but I imagine that relief is how I would look forward to going to buy something to eat on the bus home, where nobody would know or see. Buying the right food was essential – if I bought the 'wrong' thing or something new and it didn't 'work', I would have to go back and do it all over again until I got the right taste and texture and could sink into that zombie trance and switch off.

I was desperate to stop craving food, so I paid for gastric band hypnotherapy but I kept falling asleep in the sessions and I forgot about the last one. A few years before my ADHD diagnosis, I had spoken to my local mental health team about a resurgence of depression in an effort to be a grown-up and perhaps sort out some therapy. I was genuinely surprised when they referred me to the local psychiatric hospital, where I was diagnosed with binge eating disorder (BED). As a teenager, I'd naively tried to become anorexic to make myself smaller in size, if not in height, but my food cravings and the watchful eye of my mum made that impossible. I knew how unhealthy it was not to eat but couldn't reconcile that with bingeing, so I squirrelled that knowledge out of sight and out of mind. How bloody typical that I'd given myself an eating disorder without noticing. I thought that recovery would be something that just happened, like switching on a light. Even the term made me think of it as being distanced from me, possibly happening in another room, and I would then welcome that person back like a new handbag and carry on with life but lighter, healthier, more dignified – better. Whenever I started putting on weight after bingeing, it was almost a relief because, finally, I thought I looked as disgusting as I did in my head. I had ingrained the idea that it was only acceptable to be very tall if you were also a model size. Now people could see what a bad person I was just for not fitting in my clothes; a giant pudding waiting for someone to notice how miserable I was yet how content to be miserable because it was what I deserved. In order to recover, I had to surrender, but I was so busy struggling to be perfect that I couldn't acknowledge that I was still, after all these years, broken.

Outpatient treatment was a mixed bag. I couldn't master meal planning and found writing food diaries and thus facing the reality of what I was eating deeply upsetting. Documenting specific measures was too intense, and I would get utterly overwhelmed; apps like MyFitnessPal can be great, but not for me. But I learned the crucial difference between comfort eating and bingeing, which I have kept hold of since. Thanks to therapy, exploring ADHD and listening to a lot of podcasts, I don't binge any more. Shahroo Izadi's book *The Last Diet* was so helpful that I bought multiple copies for people on my Instagram who'd asked to read it. I still go to town on cereal and chocolate at certain times of my menstrual cycle or if the weather is particularly grey, but those zombie trances don't happen now. I think partly it's because I'm more accepting of myself, so I'm not keeping secrets and don't need those protections. I also find it easier to eat less crap if I'm having regular meals, which is more likely if I have frequent time away. A week into a change of scene, and it's like I've got new batteries. I always forget that even though it always happens, and once more, nine months will have passed, and I'm wondering why the world is ending.

Lotta Borg Skoglund talks more about preparing yourself for what happens regularly in the chapter on hormones. As well as holidays and my period, I need to prepare for intense afternoon cravings during colder months, even though this will only be a couple of hours after my afternoon meds. Whereas I would once have torn a strip off myself for not being happy with twelve almonds or whatever mad specific nonsense the diet books suggest, now I know that sometimes I'll have a meal, and sometimes I'm just going to have the craved snack. Bag of Pretzel Flipz, is it? Fine. This is just the time I'm in. This is all right compared to any number of other things it could be. They're not going to ruin my day. The ADHD diagnosis set off an instant light bulb regarding food, and simply knowing about it has helped with my eating habits and what can set off cravings. Alcohol was a different matter. I've made my peace with not drinking again. Two weeks after I finished writing this book, I finally said goodbye to coffee, too. There are plenty of marvellous things in this world that I am not hooked on, and I'm ready to focus on those instead.

JAMES, 47: I don't do drugs and very rarely drink because I don't like it, but the benefit that it has is it stops you from getting bored. Boredom is almost my greatest fear in all things. I remember thinking if I ever committed a crime and went to prison, the thing that would kill me would be the boredom – just the thought of being sat there with nothing to do. I surround myself with books, TV shows and films. It felt like I spent my entire life preparing for the pandemic, creating this bunker of entertainment so that I didn't need anything from the outside world and could keep my brain occupied indefinitely.

Even thinking about not having anything to do makes me anxious. It's slightly painful. If I walk to the shops, I have to have a podcast. I have to have something going at all times to keep me entertained. From what I've read about ADHD, that thirst for dopamine can be really fucking damaging. It's not just, 'Oh, I'm going to call a friend,' you can go down some dark paths; the need for dopamine is constant, so it's trying to find an outlet that isn't going to give you cholesterol or an STD or get you arrested, you know? For me, it's *Battlestar Galactica*, fiction and things like that, but it is a movable feast. It's a constantly evolving battle to find ways of navigating this.

EMILY, 48: I've never hugely self-medicated, that I'm aware of anyways, but I know people who have felt a lot of grief during the diagnosis process because they suddenly understood why. Self-medication can sometimes be so destructive, but you can't stop doing it because you need the level of functioning it gives you. When I was younger, that was probably sex and dating. My self-medicating was that constant dopamine.

SEAN, 38: I feel like there's this ADHD lottery: what will you get into? In my case, it's biscuits and video games. I'm borderline diabetic, and I'm not in very good shape because exercise is not one of the things that lights my brain up. Even at fifteen, I knew that when I get into things, I really get into them, so I was pretty sure that if I started drinking, that would be a bad time. I know people with ADHD who've had cocaine addiction but don't want to play video games because they know they'll waste too much time. I feel like I've got relatively lucky in that sense, but I find it really interesting that, even pre-diagnosis, people with ADHD recognise that trait within themselves.

ANNABELLE, 51: Going through the ADHD diagnosis was much harder than Step Four in AA because I had to go into it and trace my way back. I've used every single coping mechanism – drugs, alcohol and relationships – to fill the hole in the soul that I never knew was there. I used to eat for comfort, but furtively. My mum's whole thing was, 'You can never be too thin', all that kind of childhood stuff.

I went to boarding school and loved it. I didn't have people telling me off, it was all girls, and we all looked after each other. I didn't have any issues making friends, but there was always something I just couldn't put my finger on. I didn't realise then, but when I was about seventeen, I had a bit of a breakdown. Everything's brushed under the carpet in my family, so I was taken somewhere to recover, and it's all been denied ever since. But that was the first instance, and then I've always muddled along.

I went out and had a gastric bypass through that impulsiveness, and because I couldn't eat, I had no way to self-comfort. I'd always been a drinker, but it escalated to the point that, within three years, I was street homeless. I'd walked out on an eighteen-year marriage. Everything fell apart. I did the whole rounds: day programmes and detoxes. I cannot tell you how many times. I think I did seven rehabs. I'd plough through to the end, then a couple of days before I was due to go home, I knew that I wouldn't be able to manage, so I'd go out and relapse. When I walked out of my marriage, I went to live in a hostel. I was insane, I thought, with the drink. A few months afterwards, I had to move into a flat. It was the first time I'd ever been by myself, and I was so overwhelmed that I woke up in a psychiatric hospital. Again, I just brushed that under the carpet.

I was in hospitals for nearly a year, but I'd come straight back out. After my first diagnosis of chronic cirrhosis, where I'd lost 70 per cent of my liver, I still went back out and drank. It was the impulsiveness and the recklessness of it. My last drink was at a rehab I'd been to before. That first time, I'd found it too strict and was doing it to get everyone off my back and keep everyone happy. I never realised it, but I thrive under structure. Left to my own devices, I'll be sitting on YouTube or googling Philip Schofield until next Thursday. Sobriety was amazing for the first three or four years while I learned how to do everything again. Then I'd see my peers from around the same time getting sober and manageable, whereas I just couldn't. I can mask with the best of them, but inside, I asked, 'What the fuck is wrong with me?'

When I was finally diagnosed, I was eight years sober. I was 100 per cent up for trying the medication – I was curious! – but what they don't tell you when you go for the NHS diagnosis is that it can take up to two years to get the funding, so it was like, 'Oh God, what do I do now?' Working in substance misuse, I saw so many clients that I seemed to gravitate towards naturally, fellow ADHDers without even knowing it. I felt I was in a really difficult position because I had people coming in for their addiction problems. The last thing I wanted to do was to go, 'Have you heard of ADHD?' and land another huge thing on them, so I thought, 'I'm going to start an AA meeting specifically for neurodivergent people.'

It was organic in that ADHD way: got a date, did some research, got the word out there. We're in week ten now, and more and more people are coming. Having a community where we can laugh, embrace our awkwardness and actually feel proud is so important. God, we all know that it's bloody hard. I don't go down the victim hole or anything, but it is, and being in a community of other mad addicts who have ADHD was the final piece in the jigsaw I've been looking for my entire life. It took me ten years to get sober, to 'get it', to understand the impulsiveness, the fuck-it button, the just being able to walk away from it. So many guys from prison have got ADHD and have never been treated, along with untreated alcoholism, depression, anxiety and all the other comorbidities. Nobody talks about it, but how could they not in a drug service? There's a conversation that needs to be had about interventions that could be made at these points for people not to have to go down where we've been.

CLARE, 42: We used to stop drinking every January; a group of friends and I would always do it for charity. The last time we did it, I just never restarted. That's one of the things that made my ADHD symptoms or traits more noticeable and led me to get a diagnosis. I didn't drink a lot, maybe once a week, a bottle of Crémant or whatever, a couple of gins. It wasn't like I was drinking every night or binge drinking, but my anxiety would worsen after I'd had a drink. In hindsight, even that was enough to get that little bit of dopamine, so when I did stop, my anxiety got better – brilliant – but it made everything else come to the forefront.

I'm pickier with where I go now; it needs to be with people I want to spend more time with. If you have a few drinks, you'll make idle chitchat with people if you have to, but I don't want to now. If I've gone away for girls' weekends, I've said I'm going to the room early to read or give myself time alone. Everyone's been like, 'Yeah, absolutely fine.' I went to a hen party a couple of weeks ago and was first to bed each night. Nobody minded. They probably didn't even notice! It's needing to have an escape route. Before, maybe I would grin and bear it a little bit longer. I'll have one more drink. Whereas now I don't need to. I'm home and in my pyjamas by ten, and happy about that.

THE PROFESSIONAL VIEW

SHAHROO IZADI: The question of why some people become addicted to things is often thrown up in the air. I don't think anyone should have a hard and fast answer – I know that's annoying, but there are too many variables. When it comes to food, most of my clients binge to tap out. It's almost like they accidentally learned that from dieting. Going from a scarcity mindset to a last hurrah, they found a numbing component that could be used to think less about their problems.

Then, there's that 'I've blown it' mentality when one error turns into a total spiral, which is very common and means you're white-knuckling things. They don't trust themselves to take common-sense advice when plans don't go to plan. They take the worst possible advice as a reinforcement, 'I was never going to be able to do this anyway. I'm not the sort of person who can be like that.' There's a rebellion component, which I think people find quite exciting.

It's not just missing the dopamine hits and sugar and all that stuff we know you can get from food when they stop. They miss the planning, the feeling that they will be a new person and everything will be different. And then, very interestingly, I find, they mourn the identity of it. 'What am I now, some boring person who just eats vegetables?' When people who've given up alcohol come to see me about binge eating, they say, 'Well, if I give up this as well, then what do I have?' Not just in terms of a coping strategy for boredom, anxiety, stress or low mood or reward, but also in terms of fun: 'I like to think of myself as a fun person who does fun stuff. And now I'm the sort of person who has to worry about and be moderate with this, as well?' That comes up for a lot of women.

You need to *want* to gain that trust in yourself. For a lot of my clients, it's about wanting to feel mature and clever, the same way they do in the rest of their lives. Many of the women I speak to do extraordinary things; they are respected and consider themselves a safe pair of hands, but regarding how they behave in secret, especially around food – which isn't taken seriously enough – they feel stupid, immature and weak. So, if it's making common-sense moderate decisions around foods that bring that part of their lives up to meet the rest of it, many of them find that quite a compelling task. Whenever things aren't going to plan with food, one of my clients thinks, 'What's the most mature and intelligent choice that I can make right now?' That's also completely changed things for her in other areas.

When things are on heavy rotation, we build a tolerance to them – even sugar. Diversify your tools if one thing has been doing the heavy lifting for a long time. Look at all these things as solutions and ask, 'What problem am I trying to solve, and can I reduce my need for a solution to this problem?' If you're doing something because of stress, don't worry about the habit; reduce your stress so your need for the solution decreases. You don't get better at drinking or eating chocolate; you do at walking and scheduling time to talk to that friend who makes you laugh. It doesn't feel like it has a profound effect in the moment, but over time, it becomes something with real substance in your life. I've had a lot of clients, me included, who'll spend time with wider family and notice, 'Oh, I haven't seemed to want a dessert today,' or are smoking less. Ultimately, we live in the Western world, and things are boring, we don't have enough stuff to do, and we're not connected – that's a bigger issue.

Cheatsheet: How do you know if you have a problem?

DO YOU WANT TO STOP?

You are an adult: you know the recommended limits on alcohol and smoking, what a nutritionally balanced diet looks like in the abstract, and what you need to do to be healthy. You don't need this book to tell you that. If you want permission to go and seek help – here it is. Please, take it.

If you want to stop, you can speak to someone you can trust. If that feels too much, look up a recovery group near you. Or start small: look up a hashtag on Instagram or search Reddit.

PUBLIC HEALTH SUPPORT

Your GP can refer you to a treatment programme. Your country will also have individual drug and alcohol agencies whose websites collate phone numbers and actions to take.

> **England:** Talk to Frank
> **Scotland:** Know the Score
> **Wales:** Dan 24/7
> **Northern Ireland:** Public Health Agency

SUPPORT GROUPS

There's a recovery saying that 'the opposite of addiction is connection'. Mutual aid support groups often play a crucial role in overcoming addiction, compulsions and behaviours, and in enjoying a more peaceful life. They are also easy to access worldwide, whether in person or online, and are generally free, with a small donation recommended at each meeting.

A 2018 study[14] found that Women for Sobriety, LifeRing, and SMART Recovery were as effective as 12-step programmes in helping people reach and keep their sobriety in the long term.

---

14 'A Longitudinal Study of the Comparative Efficacy of Women for Sobriety, LifeRing, SMART Recovery, and 12-step Groups for those with AUD', Sarah E. Zemore, et al. https://www.ncbi.nlm.nih.gov/pmc/articles/PMC5884451/

12-STEP PROGRAMMES

The above groups were originally set up to provide a secular alternative to 12-step programmes, which use God in their language as a shorthand for 'a power greater than ourselves'. Over the decades, this has settled into whatever external force the person feels comfortable with. It often stands for Great Outdoors and Good Orderly Direction.

12-step programmes originated with Alcoholics Anonymous in 1935, and there are now specific meetings covering alcohol, narcotics, sex, codependent relationships, gambling, debt, internet and technology, food, disordered eating and nicotine. There are further types of meetings for specific addictions within those groups.

Also helpful are Al-Anon, a group for friends and relatives of alcoholics, and ACA (Adult Children of Alcoholics and Dysfunctional Families), which supports people raised in alcoholic families and other levels of dysfunction.

Proven ways to rest and recharge

- Change your scene.
- Get outside, then get outside further. Surround yourself with greenery.
- Give yourself a manageable list of things to tick off.
- Do something you loved when you were a child.
- Do something with no expectation of being good at it.

- Find a regular in-person group: writers, ADHD support, recovery, choir, pub chat, Maker Space, ParkRun.

- Become a regular somewhere you love.

- Leave your phone in another room while you sleep. (If you use it for sleep stories, use a different device instead.)

- If you cannot physically leave your phone, buy a Kitchen Safe lock box which will not open until the countdown reaches zero (thekitchensafe.com, thank you Nicole Cliffe). It works, somehow – an odd magic.

CHAPTER FOURTEEN

Onwards

What would you like to say to someone realising they have ADHD?

PHIL, 45: Welcome to the club! It's huge, has branches everywhere, and membership has its perks. Being a bit more serious, it tracks really closely with feminist theory. Realising that, even before you were born, you've been shaped by practices and institutions that men have almost entirely constructed around how they think and act is pretty mind-blowing. To discover that, even as a man, you don't think like most of those men is a shift it'll take some time to get used to. Realising you have ADHD is a good thing. We all see the world differently, but knowing that some fundamental differences are more nature than nurture can be a comfort. Finding out that other people share that exact difference, even more so.

NATASZA, 44: Take some deep breaths and let it sink in. The knowledge from your diagnosis can be very empowering and help you to unlock the support that can help you thrive, but remember, it's an adjustment, and be kind to yourself.

BETHAN, 42: Welcome to the rest of your life. Everything will be better now. Everything will make sense. You'll have a month or two post-diagnosis where you will want to cheer, dance for joy, flip a table with rage, punch the air and weep with grief all at the same time. These feelings will pass, and you'll come to accept things. You'll grieve for Old You, the unfairness and the things other people said about you, but mostly what you said to yourself. You'll apologise to yourself for who you were. I found hugging myself really helpful. Mostly, you will feel so much lighter. You'll be so much kinder to yourself. You'll forgive yourself for the things you can't do, and you'll let yourself stop trying to do them and beating yourself up about why you can't. Life will still be hard in some ways, but you will find your way and your tribe. ADHDers move in packs, and we don't even know it. You'll find the tools you need to get by; you'll work out how to protect yourself and forecast your triggers because you have the knowledge now. You'll be so much happier and I can't wait for you to really know this.

ANNA, 43: The constant distraction is annoying, and it's really hard to focus, but this can give you advantages.

My favourite is being able to follow a conversation with someone while eavesdropping on the table next door.

PETE, 51: You've been playing life on a higher difficulty setting without realising. Well done on getting this far.

EVA, 47: You probably already know a lot of the stuff that helps. Now you can refine those things and give yourself permission to work and live in a way that is most useful for you, rather than thinking you're deficient and constantly trying to fit yourself into the 'normal' box.

HUW, 43: It's going to be a bit of a slog, and some things might never get to the point where they're as easy as they are for other people, but knowing that your brain works differently is half the battle.

JADE, 34: A diagnosis doesn't change who you are or the things you experience, but it is so helpful in understanding some of those things. And like anything else, once you have a better understanding of something, you are better empowered to manage it.

ALICE, 40: You weren't a bad person, or lazy, or whatever they said. Your brain is just a lovely poodle, not a lovely Labrador.

LIZZIE, 29: Grief is natural, but you are who you've always been. You are now able to be kind to yourself. You've not failed; you've evolved. Maybe you're magic just how you are, and maybe there will be ways life can be less awful.

SARAH, 35: I hope you're okay. Process it in your own time. Be kind to yourself – really kind. I found I was sad for the younger me and how hard I was on her.

FRANCINE, 53: Breathe. Give yourself time to grieve. Then, enjoy getting to understand the world from a different perspective.

RADHIKA, 18: You finally have an answer to your feelings. There will be hard days, but you will find ways to cope!

MATTHEW, 10: Don't worry. Just make sure your parents and teachers are aware and try and get them to inform a doctor. Try and do lots of exercise and brain work to try and help you; for instance, I dance and play cricket. Don't worry that, as far as you know, there's nobody in history who had ADHD. There will have been; they just didn't realise ADHD was a thing.

EMMA, 34: It doesn't change anything about you; it just helps you understand yourself better, and that power and clarity cannot be underestimated.

JULIA, 45: It's not the end of the world. You are not a broken horse; you are a marvellous unicorn.

DEBBY, 35: You aren't alone. I was simultaneously angry and elated when I started reading about it, and the puzzle pieces clicked into place. I'd internalised all the blame for the consequences of my symptoms for decades, and suddenly finding a reason was overwhelming. But it does get better. Learning about the condition and about yourself and how your brain works is the first step in finding ways to make life better for yourself.

ALISON, 51: Be kind to yourself. You are awesome. This is not a weakness; it is just a truth.

CAROLINE, 49: Take time to process; it will take a while. Look at your family members, see who you think might also have ADHD or autism, and help them. Look at your friends; they probably all have ADHD too! Tell your boss and colleagues when you're ready and ask for accommodations once you figure out what helps you. Take the extra time, take the time out, and take the medication. Advocate for yourself and others. Drop it into a conversation – it's guaranteed other people have been wondering about themselves. Educate yourself and go with the flow; everyone's ADHD is different.

JACKIE, 45: Deep breaths. Lots of things will now make sense, and you will have lots of questions and concerns. Find support in the ADHD community. If you've got this far without being diagnosed, you are so strong, and things will get easier when you have a better understanding of yourself. Give yourself lots of kindness. Sending love.

LUCY, 47: This is a door to understanding yourself in the most wonderful way. Joining social media communities will help you see those frustrating quirks in other ADHDers, bring you acceptance, and sometimes make you laugh out loud!

CAROLINE, 35: Learn how to make it work for you. Learn about hacks to help you with things you want to achieve where ADHD is holding you back. Embrace the parts of yourself that you like and find ways to understand and accept what you don't like so much about your ADHD brain (like always being late or up against a deadline!). Be open with friends, family and partners about what your experience is like and try to use your understanding to make things friendlier, kinder and less stressful. See if brown noise helps or a certain frequency of music, explore setting timers, writing lists or creating healthy meal plans to avoid missing meals and help you build a lifestyle that supports your health and happiness.

LYDIA, 23: It's shit and difficult, but get a diagnosis. If that's not accessible, watch a lot of YouTube: there are some great channels that have much better advice than I could ever give. I'm sorry you had to live with this for so long without knowing.

ANSHUL, 27: You are not weird, and you weren't acting out at school. All ADHD means is that your brain is wired differently than most. It will bring out your best traits more. It's a scary journey, but thankfully, it's a lot less so now than when I was a kid. Knowing you have ADHD will make a lot of your life make sense, and it was very relieving for me.

HELEN, 45: Read and learn. Find Instagram accounts about ADHD and ASD, as the community is wonderful and supportive and will help so much. If you can afford it, get a private diagnosis. Remember that you are likely to spend more on self-medicating, impulse spending, fines, lost promotions, and so on, over the three-plus years you wait for an NHS diagnosis than the diagnosis and meds will cost.

HELEN, 43: Welcome to the club! I love how neurodivergent people congratulate each other when we realise, whilst others say they're sorry.

SOPHIE, 44: Be kind to yourself. Talk about it as much as you can and feel comfortable with it, and you will find others like you who can help guide you through it. You are very much not alone. If someone isn't supportive, or says they don't believe in it, just step away from them, even if temporarily.

LAUREN, 26: Don't get wrapped up in 'fixing' yourself right away. Your ADHD is inherently a part of you and not something that needs to be fixed. It's worth taking some time to understand which facets of your life it impacts and how these can be positive or negative before taking action. You've made it this far – congrats! – so it's okay to take your time with the next steps and consider all the options.

NAOMI, 26: I would stress the importance of a support system. I know that I personally wouldn't be able to do life if it weren't for people I can talk to about my problems and who are willing and happy to help in whichever way they can. It's just such an important factor, firstly, emotionally, to not feel isolated. But secondly, to not let yourself fall into a black hole of not being able to manage life, especially as you grow up and we're expected to be independent, take care of ourselves, and do all of these things that everyone just gets done, but which in many ways are genuinely limited by our capacity.

Remember that if you can't walk, you have a ramp and a wheelchair. You deserve to be treated in a way that's fair. The world is built for neurotypical people – that doesn't mean that's the best way for it to be built, just the most convenient – but you're not an inconvenience for needing what you need. If anything, flip it: they're the ones who are being inconvenient because there was no need for everything to go this way! People need to know more about ADHD because it's just being brushed off as quirkiness when it affects every fucking aspect of your life.

Author's note

It's always fun to look at research for evidence that, rather than something being fashionable, it's usually social change that has led to it being more clearly seen. When something gets in the way of productivity, society will finally decide to address it. ADHD in children is far more accepted in Western culture now, but the traits were only identified in the West in the late eighteenth century when children started being treated as individuals in their own right.

It is impossible not to identify ADHD traits once you learn about it. From a passing remark from the charismatic, corrupt Falstaff in Henry IV Part II ('It is the disease of not listening, the malady of not marking, that I am troubled withal') to L.M. Montgomery's equally classic Anne and Emily books from centuries later, it becomes very tempting to retroactively diagnose people, whether real or fictional. Anne Shirley in Anne of Green Gables – combined. Emily Starr in Emily of New Moon – inattentive. Ilse Crawford and Mr Carpenter, also in the Emily series, clearly hyperactive-impulsive. Lorelai Gilmore in Gilmore Girls is textbook hyperactive-impulsive; Sookie is combined; Rory is – just very deeply boring. I have lost hours on research journal websites reading papers where diagnostic criteria establish ADHD symptoms in Leonardo da Vinci; the subjects of Jan Steen's 1670 painting, The Village School, and yes, Lucy Maud Montgomery and her characters. I've found that if reading other people's experiences and expertise hasn't yet quietened the worries in your head, it can be comforting to pummel yourself gently but consistently with hard facts. Many people I interviewed pointed me to researchers or concepts I hadn't heard of.

Professor Philip Asherson introduced me to consensus statements, where researchers review scientific papers across a similar topic to produce empirically correct statements. The most recent worldwide consensus statement on ADHD, led by Stephen V. Faraone in 2021, found 208 evidence-based conclusions about a condition some people still try to call a fad, or not real, or the consequence of too many E-numbers. Faraone's statement was approved by eighty authors from twenty-seven countries and six continents and endorsed by a further 366 people. Your brain may still try to persuade you that you are the exception and that you need to try harder. You don't.

Cheatsheet: Summary of findings from The World Federation of ADHD International Consensus Statement

- The syndrome we now call ADHD has been described in the medical literature since 1775.[15]

- When made by a licensed clinician, the diagnosis of ADHD is well defined and valid at all ages, even in the presence of other psychiatric disorders, which is common.

15 'The World Federation of ADHD International Consensus Statement: 208 Evidence-based conclusions about the disorder', Stephen V. Faraone etc., 2021, https://www.sciencedirect.com/science/article/pii/S014976342100049X?via%3Dihub

- ADHD is more common in males and occurs in 5.9 per cent of youth and 2.5 per cent of adults. It has been found in studies from Europe, Scandinavia, Australia, Asia, the Middle East, South America and North America.

- ADHD is rarely caused by a single genetic or environmental risk factor but most cases of ADHD are caused by the combined effects of many genetic and environmental risks each having a very small effect.

- Neuroimaging studies find small differences in the structure and functioning of the brain between people with and without ADHD. These differences cannot be used to diagnose ADHD.

- People with ADHD are at increased risk for obesity, asthma, allergies, diabetes mellitus, hypertension, sleep problems, psoriasis, epilepsy, sexually transmitted infections, abnormalities of the eye, immune disorders and metabolic disorders.

- People with ADHD are at increased risk for low quality of life, substance use disorders, accidental injuries, educational underachievement, unemployment, gambling, teenage pregnancy, difficulties socialising, delinquency, suicide and premature death.

- Studies of economic burden show that ADHD costs society hundreds of billions of dollars each year, worldwide.

- Regulatory agencies around the world have determined that several medications are safe and effective for reducing the symptoms of ADHD as shown by randomised controlled clinical trials.

- Treatment with ADHD medications reduces accidental injuries, traumatic brain injury, substance abuse, cigarette smoking, educational underachievement, bone fractures, sexually transmitted infections, depression, suicide, criminal activity and teenage pregnancy.

- The adverse effects of medications for ADHD are typically mild and can be addressed by changing the dose or the medication.

- Non-medication treatments for ADHD are less effective than medication treatments for ADHD symptoms but are frequently useful to help problems that remain after medication has been optimised.

You don't know what you don't know. But now you know for sure: it's not a bloody trend.

Resources

Books

ADHD 2.0 by Edward M. Hallowell and John J. Ratey, John Murray Press, 2023

ADHD: An A–Z by Leanne Maskell, Jessica Kingsley Publishers, 2022

ADHD Girls to Women: Getting on the Radar by Lotta Borg Skoglund, Jessica Kingsley Publishers, 2023

Better Late Than Never by Emma Mahony, Welbeck Publishing Group Limited, 2021

Dirty Laundry by Richard Pink and Roxanne Emery, Vintage Publishing, 2023

Earthed by Rebecca Schiller, Elliott & Thompson Ltd, 2021

Laziness Does Not Exist by Devon Price, Atria Books, 2021

Scatter Brain by Shaparak Khorsandi, Ebury Publishing, 2023

Understanding ADHD in Girls & Women by Joanne Steer, Jessica Kingsley Publishers, 2021

Unmasked by Ellie Middleton, Penguin Lite, 2023

Podcasts

ADHD As Females

ADHD Experts – If you only listen to one podcast, make it this one. Skip the first five minutes of introductory throat-clearing.

ADHD for Smart Ass Women

I Have ADHD

Is It My ADHD?

Life with Lost Keys

International organisations, support groups and communities

ADDA (add.org/adda-virtual-programs); ADDers (adders.org.uk) – both feature support groups listed by identity and country

ADDitude (additudemag.com) – articles, podcasts and twenty-five years of content from this quarterly magazine, available digitally to international subscribers

ADHD Babes (adhdbabes.com)

ADHD for Smart Ass Women (https://www.facebook.com/groups/1541724249266515/)

NeuroQueer (neuroqueer.org)

Reddit (reddit.com) has excellent country- and identity-specific ADHD communities

Sistas With ADHD (sistaswithadhd.com)

Channels and content creators

ADHD Alien (Pina Varnel)

ADHD Jesse (Jesse Anderson)

ADHD Love (Richard Pink and Roxanne Emery)

Adulting ADHD (Rach Idowu)

Black Girl, Lost Keys (René Brooks)

Brave Dave (David Frank)

Connor DeWolfe

Dani Donovan

Geraint Works (Geraint Evans)

How To ADHD (Jessica McCabe)

The Mini ADHD Coach (Alice Gendron)

Struggle Care/Domestic Blisters (KC Davis)

Documentaries

The Disruptors (2022)

Free The Mind (2012)

ADHD traits in popular culture

TV:

30 Rock; Bluey; Bob's Burgers; Brooklyn 99; Buffy the Vampire Slayer; Community; Crazy Ex-Girlfriend; Doctor Who; Friends; Futurama; Gilmore Girls; House; How I Met Your Mother; I Love Lucy; Malcolm in the Middle; Marvel Rising: Secret Warriors; Miranda; Modern Family; Ms Marvel; New Amsterdam; New Girl; Parks and Recreation; Peep Show; Psych; Red Dwarf; Sailor Moon; Scrubs; Spaced; Steven Universe; Stranger Things; Teen Wolf; The Little House on the Prairie; The Office (US); The Simpsons; The Sopranos; The Wind in the Willows; Tuca and Bertie.

Film:

Ace Ventura: Pet Detective; Back to the Future; Deadpool; Everything Everywhere All at Once; Finding Nemo; Frozen; Iron Man; Julie & Julia; Mrs Doubtfire; So Damn Easy Going; The Peanut Butter Falcon; The Sound of Music; Thumbsucker; Uncut Gems; anything starring Jack Black.

Books:

Act Your Age, Eve Brown by Talia Hibbert; All The Feels by Olivia Dade; Anne of Green Gables by L. M. Montgomery; Armadale by Wilkie Collins; Blackbirds by Chuck Wendig; Bridget Jones's Diary by Helen Fielding; Calvin and Hobbes by Bill Watterson; Emily of New Moon by L. M. Montgomery; Hyperbole and a Half by Allie Brosh; Percy Jackson and the Olympians by Rick Riordan; Pippi Longstocking by Astrid Lindgren; Red, White & Royal Blue by Casey McQuiston; Scott Pilgrim's Precious Little Life by Bryan Lee O'Malley; The Complete Sherlock Holmes by Arthur Conan Doyle; Six of Crows by Leigh Bardugo, Joey Pigza Swallowed the Key by Jack Gantos; The Extraordinaries by T. J. Klune; The Hitchhiker's Guide to the Galaxy by Douglas Adams; The Stormlight Archives by Brandon Sanderson; The Wind in the Willows by Kenneth Grahame; Unsheltered by Barbara Kingsolver.

Acknowledgements

This book came together quickly but was years in the researching. Thank you to the podcasters and scientists who have helped me understand what is going on in my head. To everyone whose lives I have negatively impacted, I'm truly sorry. To everyone who has negatively impacted mine: suck it.

Thank you to every ADHDer who gave me their time, support and humour with such generosity. Thank you also to Professor Susan Young, Professor Ellie Dommett, Dr Shyamal Mashru, Dr Tony Lloyd, Professor Philip Asherson, Dr Louise Newson, Lotta Borg Skoglund, Jenn Jordan, Bethan Davies, Dr Sarah Cannon-Gibbs, Cat Harris and Shahroo Izadi, for your kindness and expertise and for helping so many people.

For my agent, Millie Hoskins, for her kindness, patience and forbearance and for making all my dreams come true. To Andrew McAleer at Robinson, who instantly 'got' this book (and took Millie and me to lunch!) and gave me sensible and sensitive edits, and unending support, even in the face of a 23-page PowerPoint deck about what I did and did not want from an ADHD book cover. To Duncan Spilling and Maggie Limbu, who, faced with said PowerPoint, turned out an absolute dream cover that was perfect first time. Thank you to Amanda Keats, Sarah Thomas and Narjas Zatat for such amazing work to get it into the world.

Due to my need for self-bribery, this book was written at Lynwood & Co in Bampton and SW16 Bar & Kitchen, Estate Office Coffee and Starbucks in Streatham Hill. Thank you to Clark, Anya, Tom, Sagal, Emma and everyone who kept me so well-fed, caffeinated and cared for.

Thank you to my forest of Helens – Zaltzman, Whitaker, O'Hara – and to Annie Durham, Rachel Dobson, Victoria Glass, Ebona Eastmond-Henry and Ben De Pfeiffer-Key. To Ross Jones, Jo Elvin, Harriet Addison, Lesley Thomas and Claire Cohen for believing in my writing. To my ADHD friends on WhatsApp and Instagram – thank God for you, basically – and to Jackie, Daisy, Beth, Jo, Al, Emily, Lou and Ben, who read my book proposal and helped me to make it so much better. Thank you to the Hamilton group and the Jilly Cooper Book Club for being such legends.

To my comrades in horsey adventures – Hannah Franklin-Wallis, Claire Wright, Sarah Deverill, Lisa Noble, Megan Harrison-Lund, Fizz and Harry Shearcroft, and Emma Thomas – and especially Laura

'Dilly' Bradley, Clare Russell at Light Cavalry HAC, and Katie Kennedy, Tim Pearce-May and Pam Pearce-May at Mill Farm. Thank you for putting up with my continued crimes against equestrianism.

To Professor Tanya Byron, for so many years of reassurance before we actually spoke in person.

To my family – Jane, Richard, Nick, Suzie, Florence and Annabel; and Sarah, Nigel, Archie, Jenny, Jack, Amy, Cecily, Stuart, Clemi, Monty, Basil, Raffy, Tabitha, Ralph, Nell and Hector. Thank you for the crosswords, the jokes, the love, all of it.

Thank you to the John Radcliffe Hospital in Oxford for saving my father-in-law after he dramatically pulled focus from my book deal by spending much of spring 2023 in a coma and recovery. Nigel, I love you, and I am so glad you are now banned from ladders.

To my beloved companions Ambridge, Genevieve and Sybil – and above all, to Harry: my partner in life, animal admin, and The Times Quick Cryptic. Thank you for being so patient, kind and incredibly good-looking.

And my sincere thanks to you, the reader, without whom this book would not exist – much love to you. You've got this.

Index